teacher's friend publications

October!

a creative idea book

for the

elementary teacher

written and illustrated

by

Karen Sevaly

Copyright © Teacher's Friend,
a Scholastic Company
All rights reserved.
Printed in China.

ISBN-13 978-0-439-50378-5
ISBN-10 0-439-50378-7

This book is dedicated
to teachers and children
everywhere.

6 to 7 Kids

- Candy corn (markers) (mashmellor)
  in Snack bags

- Small gussing jar + paper (gussing paper)   prize

- 10 prizes

Small pumkin

- 3 pumpkin (long stems)

3 Stations
   10 min / Slut. → pumkinpass
   Bingo all together

Table of Contents

Making the most of it!

WHAT IS IN THIS BOOK:

You will find the following in each monthly idea book from Teacher's Friend Publications:

1. A calendar listing every day of the month with a classroom idea, and mention of special holidays and events.

2. At least four student awards to be sent home to parents.

3. Three or more bookmarks that can be used in your school library or given to students by you as "Super Student Awards."

4. Numerous bulletin board ideas and patterns pertaining to the particular month and seasonal activity.

5. Easy to make craft ideas related to the monthly holidays and special days.

6. Dozens of activities emphasizing not only the obvious holidays but also the often forgotten celebrations such as: Fire Prevention Day, Columbus Day and Halloween.

7. Creative writing pages, crossword puzzles, word finds, booklet covers, games, paper bag puppets, literature lists and much more!

8. Scores of classroom management techniques and proven methods to motivate your students to improve behavior and classroom work.

HOW TO USE THIS BOOK:

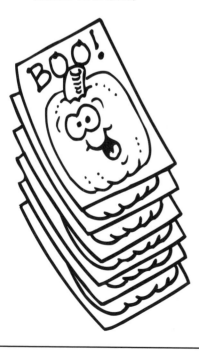

Every page of this book may be duplicated for individual classroom use.

Some pages are meant to be copied or used as duplicating masters. Other pages may be transferred onto construction paper or used as they are.

If you have access to a print shop, you will find that many pages work well when printed on index paper. This type of paper takes crayons and felt markers well and is sturdy enough to last. (Bookmarks work particularly well on index paper.)

Lastly, some pages are meant to be enlarged with an overhead or opaque projector. When we say enlarge, we mean it! Think BIG! Three, four or even five feet is great! Try using colored butcher paper or poster board so you don't spend all your time coloring.

ADDING THE COLOR:

Putting the color to finished items can be a real bother to teachers in a rush. Try these ideas:

1. On small areas, water color markers work great. If your area is rather large, switch to crayons or even colored chalk or pastels.

   (Don't worry, lamination or a spray fixative will keep color on the work and off of you. No laminator or fixative? That's okay, a little hair spray will do the trick.)

2. The quickest method of coloring large items is to start with colored paper. (Poster board, butcher paper or large construction paper work well.) Add a few dashes of a contrasting colored marker or crayon and you will have it made.

3. Try cutting character eyes, teeth, etc. from white typing paper and gluing them in place. These features will really stand out and make your bulletin boards come alive.

   For special effects, add real buttons or lace. Metallic paper looks great on stars and belt buckles, too.

LAMINATION:

If you have access to a roll laminator then you already know how fortunate you are. They are priceless when it comes to saving time and money. Try these ideas:

1. You can laminate more than just classroom posters and construction paper. Try various kinds of fabric, wallpaper and gift wrapping. You'll be surprised at the great combinations you come up with.

   Laminated classified ads can be used to cut a heading for current events bulletin boards. Colorful gingham fabric makes terrific cut letters or bulletin board trim. You might even try burlap! Bright foil gift wrapping paper will add a festive feeling to any bulletin board.

   (You can even make professional looking bookmarks with laminated fabric or burlap. They are great holiday gift ideas for mom or dad!)

2. Felt markers and laminated paper or fabric can work as a team. Just make sure the markers you use are permanent and not water-based. Oops, make a mistake! That's okay. Put a little ditto fluid on a tissue, rub across the mark and presto, it's gone! Also, dry transfer markers work great on lamination and can easily be wiped off.

LAMINATION:
(continued)

3. Laminating cut-out characters can be tricky. If you have it enlarged an illustration onto poster board, simply laminate first and then cut it out with scissors or an art knife. (Just make sure the laminator is hot enough to create a good seal.)

One problem may arise when you paste an illustration onto poster board and laminate the finished product. If your paste-up is not 100% complete, your illustration and posterboard may separate after laminating. To avoid this problem, paste your illustration onto poster board that measures slightly larger. This way, the lamination will help hold down your paste-up.

4. When pasting up your illustration, always try to use either rubber cement, artist's spray adhesive or a glue stick. White glue, tape or paste does not laminate well because it can often be seen under your artwork.

5. Have you ever laminated student-made place mats, crayon shavings, tissue paper collages, or dried flowers? You'll be amazed at the variety of creative things that can be laminated and used in the classroom or as take-home gifts.

PHOTOCOPIES AND DITTO MASTERS:

Many of the pages in this book can be copied for use in the classroom. Try some of these ideas for best results:

1. If the print from the back side of your original comes through the front when making a photocopy or ditto master, slip a sheet of black construction paper behind the sheet. This will mask the unwanted shadows and create a much better copy.

2. Several potential masters in this book contain instructions for the teacher. Simply cover the type with correction fluid or a small slip of paper before duplicating.

3. When using a new ditto master, turn down the pressure on the duplicating machine. As the copies become light, increase the pressure. This will get longer wear out of both the master and the machine.

4. Trying to squeeze one more run out of that worn ditto master can be frustrating. Try lightly spraying the inked side of the master with hair spray. For some reason, this helps the master put out those few extra copies.

MONTHLY ORGANIZERS:

Staying organized month after month, year after year can be a real challenge. Try this simple idea:

After using the loose pages from this book, file them in their own file folder labeled with the month's name. This will also provide a place to save pages from other reproducible books along with craft ideas, recipes and articles you find in magazines and periodicals. (*Essential Pocket Folders* by Teacher's Friend provide a perfect way to store your monthly ideas and reproducibles. Each *Monthly Essential Pocket Folder* comes with a sixteen-page booklet of essential patterns and organizational ideas. There are even special folders for *Back to School*, *The Substitute Teacher* and *Parent-Teacher Conferences*.)

You might also like to dedicate a file box for every month of the school year. A covered box will provide room to store large patterns, sample art projects, certificates and awards, monthly stickers, monthly idea books and much more.

BULLETIN BOARD IDEAS:

Creating clever bulletin boards for your classroom need not take fantastic amounts of time and money. With a little preparation and know-how you can have different boards each month with very little effort. Try some of these ideas:

1. Background paper should be put up only once a year. Choose colors that can go with many themes and holidays. The black butcher paper background you used as a spooky display in October will have a special dramatic effect in April with student-made, paper-cut butterflies.

2. Butcher paper is not the only thing that can be used to cover the back of your board. You might also try fabric from a colorful bed sheet or gingham material. Just fold it up at the end of the year to reuse again. Wallpaper is another great background cover. Discontinued rolls can be purchased for a small amount at discount hardware stores. Most can be wiped clean and will not fade like construction paper. (Do not glue wallpaper directly to the board, just staple or pin in place.)

3. Store your bulletin board pieces in large, flat envelopes made from two large sheets of tagboard or cardboard. Simply staple three sides together and slip the pieces inside. (Small pieces can be stored in zip-lock, plastic bags.) Label your large envelopes with the name of the bulletin board and the month and year you displayed it. Take a picture of each bulletin board display. Staple the picture to your storage envelope. Next year when you want to create the same display, you will know right where everything goes. Kids can even follow your directions when you give them a picture to look at.

LETTERING AND HEADINGS:

Not every school has a letter machine that produces perfect 4" letters. The rest of us will just have to use the old stencil and scissor method. But wait, there is an easier way!

1. Don't cut individual letters as they are difficult to pin up straight, anyway. Instead, hand print bulletin board titles and headings onto strips of colored paper. When it is time for the board to come down, simply roll it up to use again next year. If you buy your own pre-cut lettering, save yourself some time and hassle by pasting the desired statements to long strips of colored paper. Laminate if possible. These can be rolled up and stored the same way!

   Use your imagination! Try cloud shapes and cartoon bubbles. They will all look great.

2. Hand lettering is not that difficult, even if your printing is not up to penmanship standards. Print block letters with a felt marker. Draw big dots at the ends of each letter. This will hide any mistakes and add a charming touch to the overall effect.

   If you are still afraid about free handing it, try this nifty idea: Cut a strip of poster board about 28" X 6". Down the center of the strip, cut a window with an art knife measuring 20" X 2". There you have it: a perfect stencil for any lettering job. All you do is write capital letters with a felt marker within the window slot. Don't worry about uniformity. Just fill up the entire window height with your letters. Move your poster board strip along as you go. The letters will always remain straight and even because the poster board window is straight.

3. If you must cut individual letters, use construction paper squares measuring 4 1/2" X 6". (Laminate first if you can.) Cut the capital letters as shown. No need to measure, irregular letters will look creative and not messy.

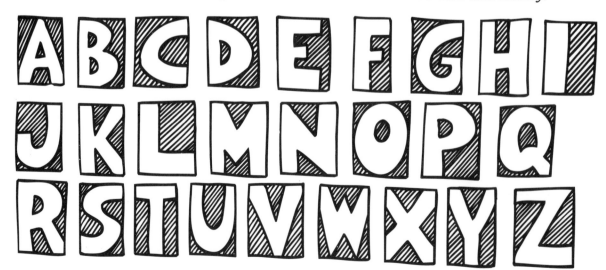

Calendar

October!

OCTOBER

1ˢᵀ The first WORLD SERIES was played on this day in 1903. (Ask class baseball fans to report the latest in baseball news.)

2ᴺᴰ MOHANDAS GANDHI, known as the "Father of India," was born on this day in 1869. (Describe Gandhi's devotion to non-violent reform to your students.)

3ᴿᴰ Today is CHILD HEALTH DAY. (Ask students to list twelve ways in which they can help to keep themselves healthy.)

4ᵀᴴ The U.S.S.R. launched the first man-made satellite, SPUTNIC, on this day in 1957. (Gather a collection of space exploration books from the school library for your students to read.)

5ᵀᴴ CHESTER A. ARTHUR, the 21st United States President, was born on this day in 1830. (Have students find out how many presidents we have had since Arthur.)

6ᵀᴴ Today is UNIVERSAL CHILDREN'S DAY. (Celebrate the occasion by reading a special story or providing a treat for your students.)

7ᵀᴴ Today is the DAY OF BREAD. (Discuss good nutrition with your class and have them sample different types of bread such as, tortillas, pita bread and bagels.)

8ᵀᴴ This day marks the birthdate of American political and religious leader JESSE JACKSON, born in 1941. (Ask students to tell you the age of Reverend Jackson.)

9ᵀᴴ Today is FIRE PREVENTION DAY. (Ask students to discuss fire safety with their parents and plan a family escape route in case of a fire in their home.)

10ᵀᴴ The people of FIJI celebrate their independence on this day. The nation of Fiji includes 300 separate islands. (Ask your students to locate them on the classroom map.)

11TH ELEANOR ROOSEVELT, American first lady and humanitarian, was born on this day in 1884. (Ask older students to find out why this particular first lady was so popular.)

12TH Today is COLUMBUS DAY. This famous Italian explorer first sighted land on this day in 1492. (Have students trace his routed from Spain to the West Indies on the classroom map.)

13TH The UNITED STATES NAVY was established on this day in 1775. (Students may like to research various naval vessels and their impact throughout our history.)

14TH The NOBEL PEACE PRIZE was awarded to Dr. Martin Luther King, Jr. on this day in 1964. (Ask students to find out about this award and how the recipients are chosen.)

15TH Today is WORLD POETRY DAY. (Have students create their own original poems. Submit the best ones to the school newspaper.)

16TH NOAH WEBSTER, creator of the American dictionary, was born on this day in 1758. (Give students five "haunting" words to locate in the class dictionary.)

17TH Today, BLACK POETRY DAY marks the birthdate of JUPITER HAMMON in 1711. He was the first published American black poet. (Find one of his poems and share it with your class.)

18TH American inventor SAMUEL MORSE laid the first telegraph cable on this day in 1842. (Have students learn to signal their names in Morse Code.)

19TH Today is YORKTOWN DAY. On this day in 1781, the last battle of the American Revolutionary War was fought. (Ask students to find Yorktown on the class map.)

20TH RINGLING BROTHERS AND BARNUM AND BAILEY CIRCUS presented "The Greatest Show On Earth" for the first time on this day in 1919. (Ask students to write a short paper about their favorite circus act.)

21ST THOMAS ALVA EDISON invented the first electric light on this day in 1879. (Have students research other Edison inventions.)

22ND FRANZ VON LISZT, the famous Hungarian pianist and composer, was born on this day in 1811. (In celebration, soothe your students with quiet classical music during free reading.)

23RD The first NATIONAL WOMEN'S RIGHTS CONVENTION was held on this day in 1850. (Ask students to describe how women's rights have changed since then.)

24TH The UNITED NATIONS was officially established on this day in 1945. (Have students select a member nation and make its flag from construction paper. Display the flags on the class bulletin board.)

25TH Famous American explorer RICHARD BYRD was born on this day in 1888. (Have students research his discovery and locate the route of his expedition on the class map.)

26TH Today is INTERNATIONAL RED CROSS DAY. (Arrange for a Red Cross volunteer to visit your classroom and discuss the various services provided by this wonderful organization.)

27TH THEODORE ROOSEVELT, the 26th United States President, was born on this day in 1858. (Ask students to locate statistical information about the president, such as years served, place of birth and age at death.)

28TH The STATUE OF LIBERTY was given to the United States by France on this day in 1886. (Ask students to bring in pictures and information about the statue and make a "Liberty" display on the class bulletin board.)

29TH The citizens of TURKEY celebrate their national independence which was proclaimed on this day in 1923. (Ask students to locate Turkey on the classroom map.)

30TH JOHN ADAMS, the 2nd United States President, was born on this day in 1735. (Ask students which president preceded Adams and which came after him.)

31ST Today is HALLOWEEN! (Remind all of your witches, ghosts and goblins about Halloween safety precautions.

TF1000 October Idea Book

October

Sunday	Monday	Tuesday	Wednesday	Thursday	Friday	Saturday

Autumn Activities!

Autumn Activities!

Autumn marks that time of year when leaves turn shades of yellow, orange and red before softly falling to the ground. The sun sets earlier each evening and a sudden chill in the air warns us that winter is just around the corner. Winds play havoc with our hair and storm clouds grow dark and gray. It's time for birds to fly south and pumpkins to ripen in the fields. It's a magic time, a time when we all discover nature's beauty.

Bring the colorful season of autumn into your classroom by having your students enjoy some of these activities.

"maple"
"oak"
"sycamore"

TREE TALK
Discuss these autumn questions with your students.

What types of trees lose their leaves?

What are the names of some of these trees?

What trees lose their leaves near your home? On the school ground?

How does a tree use its leaves?

How do animals and birds use the leaves?

LEAF STUDY
Collect enough large autumn leaves for everyone in class. Pass out one to each student. Draw a large leaf on the chalkboard and label its parts. Ask students to find these areas on their own leaves as you point them out on the board.

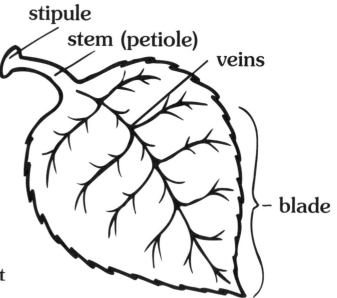

stipule
stem (petiole)
veins
- blade

BLADE - broad part of the leaf containing the food-making cells

VEINS - tiny network that moves the food product

PETIOLE - (stem) narrow channel that carries
    the food product to the tree

STIPULE - part of the stem that attaches to the tree

Autumn Activities!

LASTING LEAVES

Children will love to preserve their leaves by pressing them between sheets of waxed paper. Lay several thick pieces of newspaper on a table. Place the leaf or leaves between two sheets of waxed paper on the newspaper. Cover with more newspaper, and press with a warm iron. (Laminating autumn leaves is also very successful.) Hang the lasting leaves in a sunny window for everyone to see.

LEAF RUBBINGS

Ask each student to place his or her leaf on the desk and cover it with a piece of smooth paper.

Using the side of a crayon, children should gently rub across the leaf. Ask them to move their leaf and rub again, using a different color. Students can continue rubbing with different colors, even overlapping at times.

Display the rubbings on the class bulletin board or make booklet covers or autumn notebooks.

LEAF PAINTINGS

Primary children love to paint large, splashy abstract pictures. Give the students autumn colored tempera paint and let them paint boldly on construction paper. When the paintings are dry, trace a large leaf pattern over the paintings using a poster board stencil. Cut the leaves out and glue them to sheets of construction paper. Laminate the leaves if you wish or display them as they are.

PUMPKIN PLANTS

Save pumpkin seeds for planting later in the year. Dry the seeds on waxed paper and keep them in a small airtight container until spring.

When warm weather finally arrives, give each student a small baby food jar or pint-sized milk carton. Have the students fill the containers with soil and plant two or three pumpkin seeds. Place the containers in a sunny window and keep the soil only slightly moist. After a few weeks, each pumpkin plant will be large enough to take home to mom for a Mother's Day gift.

Autumn Activities!

LEAF STAMPS

Fall leaves make wonderful stamps for printing autumn designs. Mix autumn colors of tempera paint and ask children to gently coat one side of a leaf with the paint. Have them lay the leaf, paint side down, on a sheet of construction paper. Lift the leaf off the paper and repeat the process. The children can use one color of paint or several.

HARVEST COLLECTIONS

Ask students to collect a variety of nature's products for a class harvest display. Children will love collecting acorns, leaves, Indian corn, nuts, gourds and pumpkins. Arrange the items on a table top or in a large wicker basket. You might like to donate the display to the school office or cafeteria.

PUMPKIN FUN

Pass several small pumpkins around the classroom and ask students to examine the size, shape, texture and color of each one. Ask them to write about the pumpkins in their "Pumpkin Books" and draw detailed pictures.

PUMPKIN SEEDS

Cut the top off of one of the pumpkins while your students look on. Ask a few students to separate the seeds from the pulp. Place the seeds on a greased cookie sheet and sprinkle with salt. Roast at 350° until the seeds start to brown. Pass out a few to each student to enjoy.

PUMPKIN PUDDING

Cut a pumpkin into quarters and wrap in foil. Place in a pan and bake in the oven at 375° for about one hour. When the pumpkin has cooled, remove the outside skin and puree the pulp in an electric blender. Have the children take turns mixing the following ingredients:

3 cups of cooked pumpkin

½ t. ginger

2 beaten eggs

¼ t. cloves

1½ cups of milk

¼ t. nutmeg

1 cup of sugar

dash of salt

2 t. cinnamon

Cook the pudding in a saucepan for about 20 minutes. Continue stirring for best results. Serve the pudding in small paper cups when cool.

Autumn Activities!

TREE DISCUSSIONS

Here are a few questions about trees that you can discuss with your students:

- What are the different parts of a tree and what are their functions?
- What does a tree need in order to grow?
- How do trees benefit us?
- What benefits do animals get from trees?
- How do we know the age of trees?
- What type of trees are among the largest? The oldest?

WHY DO LEAVES CHANGE COLORS?

This question is raised in the classroom every fall. Here is a simple way to explain it to even young children.

"The green color in leaves, called chlorophyll, covers up the red, orange and yellow colors found in some kinds of leaves. When the weather turns cold, these leaves lose their chlorophyll and the bright, hot colors suddenly appear. The coldness in the air is what makes the leaves show their color, but the amount of sunshine and water also affect the color of leaves. The more cold fresh air, ample water and bright sunshine a tree has, the brighter the colors!"

SUNLIGHT LEAF PRINT

Pin a large leaf to the center of a piece of red construction paper and leave in direct sunlight for a day or more. When you remove the leaf, its print will have appeared on the paper. Ask your children: what happened to create the print?

ADOPT-A-TREE

Assign each student to select a special tree to adopt for the school year. This could be a tree in their yard at home or one they pass every day coming to school.

Begin by having each student make a tree scrapbook. In the book they should include the name of their tree, its description and a drawing or photograph. A rubbing of its bark and records of its height, as well as measurements of its trunk, should also be included. Leaves and blossoms can also be pressed and preserved in the scrapbook. Students should also list various animals and birds that use the tree for their home.

As each month goes by, have the students update the information on their tree. What changes have taken place? Do the leaves still look the same?

Tell children that they should also take some care in helping the tree to grow. They can pick up litter around the tree and perhaps water it on especially hot days.

Cut two of these trees from heavy paper and fold along the dotted lines. Staple both trees together at the folds. Fold one tree the opposite direction to make it stand on a table top. Paste red, yellow and orange bits of tissue paper to your tree to make an attractive autumn centerpiece.

Stand-Up Tree

TF1000 October Idea Book

Autumn Patterns

Use these fall patterns
as bulletin board accents
or as name tags.

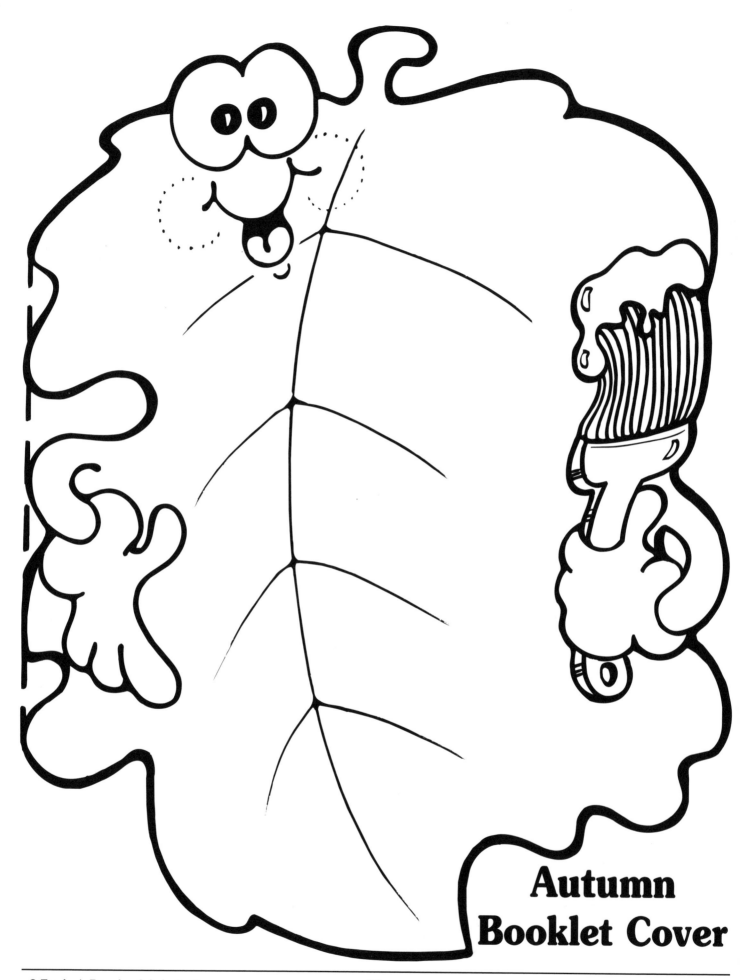

Autumn Booklet Cover

TF1000 October Idea Book

Pumpkin Booklet Cover

Copy this pattern onto a folded sheet of construction paper. Place lined writing paper inside. Cut all layers of paper at one time. Staple at the fold.

Students may write their own "Pumpkin" stories inside.

 TF1000 October Idea Book

Pencil Toppers

Reproduce these "Pencil Toppers" onto construction or index paper. Color and cut them out. Use an art knife to cut through the Xs.

Slide a pencil through both Xs, as shown.

Use as classroom awards or birthday treats.

TF1000 October Idea Book

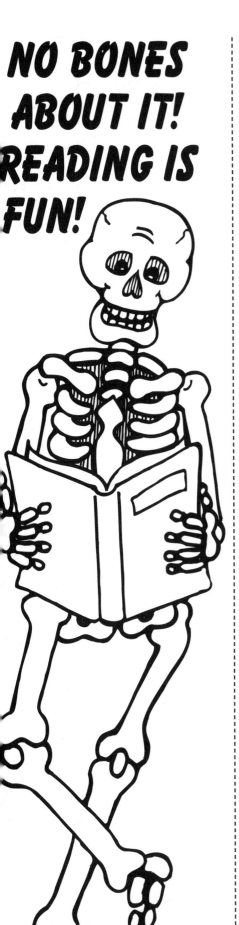

NO BONES ABOUT IT! READING IS FUN!

WISE UP!

VISIT THE LIBRARY!

Only treats, No tricks, in the Library!

CERTIFICATE

OF

RECOGNITION

presented to

NAME

in recognition of

TEACHER

DATE

STUDENT
OF THE
WEEK

NAME

SCHOOL

DATE

TEACHER

SUPER JOB!

_____
Name

_____
Date

_____
Teacher

WOW!

_____
Name

Was "Bewitching" Today!

_____

_____

_____

_____
Teacher   Date

BOO!

MUCH BETTER!

_____
Name

_____

_____

_____
Teacher   Date

_____
Name

Was A "Huge" Success Today!

_____
Teacher

_____
Date

Crow Pattern

Have each student cut these patterns from black and yellow construction paper. Display good work papers on 9" x 12" sheets of black paper and assemble the crow pieces, as shown.

Display the crows on a cut-paper fence on your bulletin board for an attractive autumn scene.

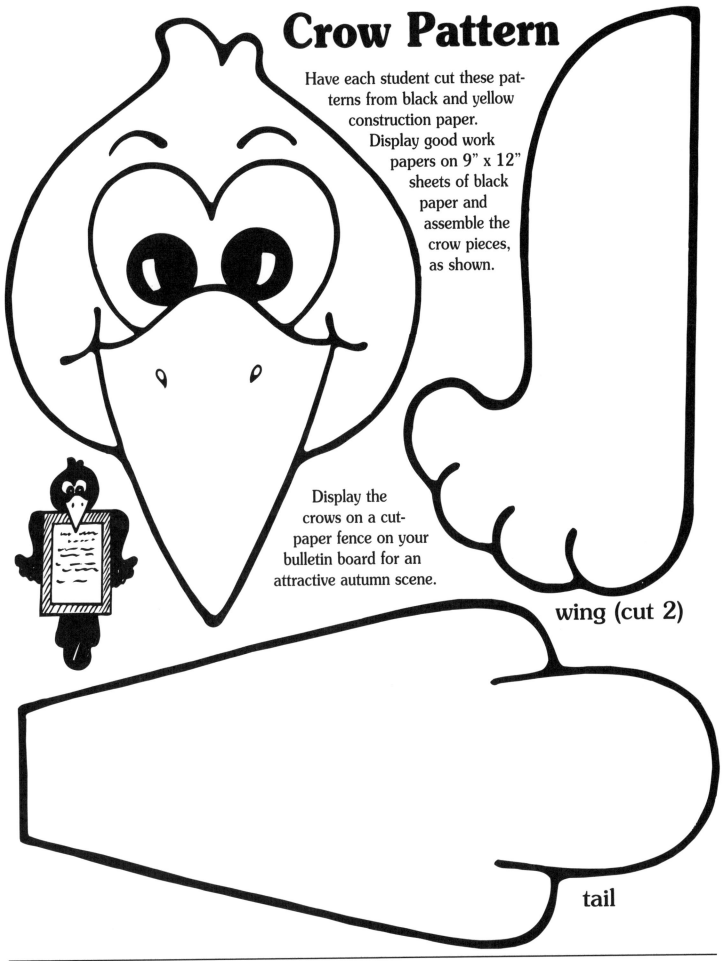

wing (cut 2)

tail

Popcorn Activities!

POPCORN BULLETIN BOARD

Give each student a wide strip of construction paper and ask them to write their names in large block letters.

As a class project, pop a large quantity of popcorn using an air popper. Give each student a paper cup full of popped corn to glue to the outline of his or her name. When dry, pin the names to the class bulletin board along with individual students' good work papers. Title the board *"Look Who's Popping!"* or *"We're Popping with Good Learning!"* Make sure you pop enough corn for munching!

POPCORN SURPRISE!

When the class has accomplished a job well done, treat the students to a popcorn surprise. Spread a large sheet in the center of the class floor. Place an air popper in the middle. Have all the students sit around the edge of sheet. Remind them that all poppers become very hot and that they should stay a safe distance away. Turn on the popper. Your children will be delighted to see the popcorn explode all over the sheet and at the same time enjoy the tasty kernels. (Make sure you have some extra popped corn ready for those students that may not have gotten as much as others.)

POPCORN WORD PLAY

Ask students to describe popcorn in a variety of ways. They may like to describe its smell, taste, and texture. They could also describe places where they most like to eat popcorn. Ask students to list descriptive words on the class board. Instruct them to use at least ten of the words in a "popcorn" poem or story. Here are a few to get you started:

HOW DOES POPCORN POP?

Native Americans believed that a small demon lived in each kernel. When his house was heated to a high temperature, the demon would get so mad he would explode!

What really happens is quite simple. Each kernel contains moisture in its soft center. When the kernel is heated to about 400° Fahrenheit the moisture turns to steam. The hard outer shell holds back the expanding steam until it finally "POPS!" The hard shell then bursts open and the fluffy center turns inside out!

munch	crunchy	crispy
buttery	puffy	warm
snack	kernels	fresh
explode	pop	salty
flavor	caramel	oil

Whooooo Me?
(owl activities!)

Owl Activities!

The ancient Greeks believed that owls represent wisdom and knowledge. Their large eyes make them look especially wise. However owls are no more intelligent than many other birds. Try one of these activities with your students.

WISE OLD OWL

Cover an empty tissue box with colorful paper and decorate with a paper-cut owl. Write on the top of the box, "Dear Wise Old Owl..."

Explain to the students that whenever they have a problem or an important question they can write to "Wise Old Owl." The situations can be real or imaginary. Assure students that they are not required to sign their names.

Several times throughout the week, pull one of the problems from the box and read it out loud to the class. Brain-storm with your students on ways the problem might be solved. You may wish to divide the class into groups and have each group report to the rest of the class.

WISE OWL MATH

Ask six students to sit in the center of a circle formed by the other students. Select one student to be the "Wise Owl." The Owl "flies" around the perimeter of the circle and stops behind one student. He or she calls out a math problem, such as; "nine times three is how much?" If one of the players in the center of the circle can shout out the answer before the challenger, the two must exchange places. If the challenged student answers first, he or she must change places with the "Wise Owl" and the game continues.

GIVE A HOOT!

The saying, "to give a hoot" means simply to "care." Ask your students what they give a "hoot" about.

Begin by listing a variety of concerns on the class board. These may include concerns that individual students might have or more universal problems such as world hunger and war. Have children select one of these concerns and instruct them to write a paper on why they "give a hoot." Tell them that just "caring" should be extended into action, such as writing a congressman or contributing to a charity?

OWL WISDOM

Owls are easy to distinguish from other types of birds. All owls have large, broad heads and many have tufts of feathers that look like ears. (Owls do have ears, they are actually hidden under their feathers.) Even though owls have large eyes and keen eyesight, their eyes can only be directed forward. To look to the side, an owl must move its entire head. Owls can even turn their heads entirely backwards!

There are many different types of owls. Ask your students to each research one the following:

Great Horned Owl	Elf Owl
Burrowing Owl	Barn Owl
Snowy Owl	Screech Owl

**Owl
Booklet
Cover**

TF1000 October Idea Book

Tape or glue a 9" x 12" sheet of construction paper into a cylinder shape.

Cut these owl patterns from heavy brown and yellow paper. Glue the patterns in place, as shown.

Fold the beak down the center. Fold back each flap and glue in place.

Fold the flap on the feet pattern and glue it to the inside of the cylinder.

Cut two wings.

Stand-Up Owl

Owl Mask

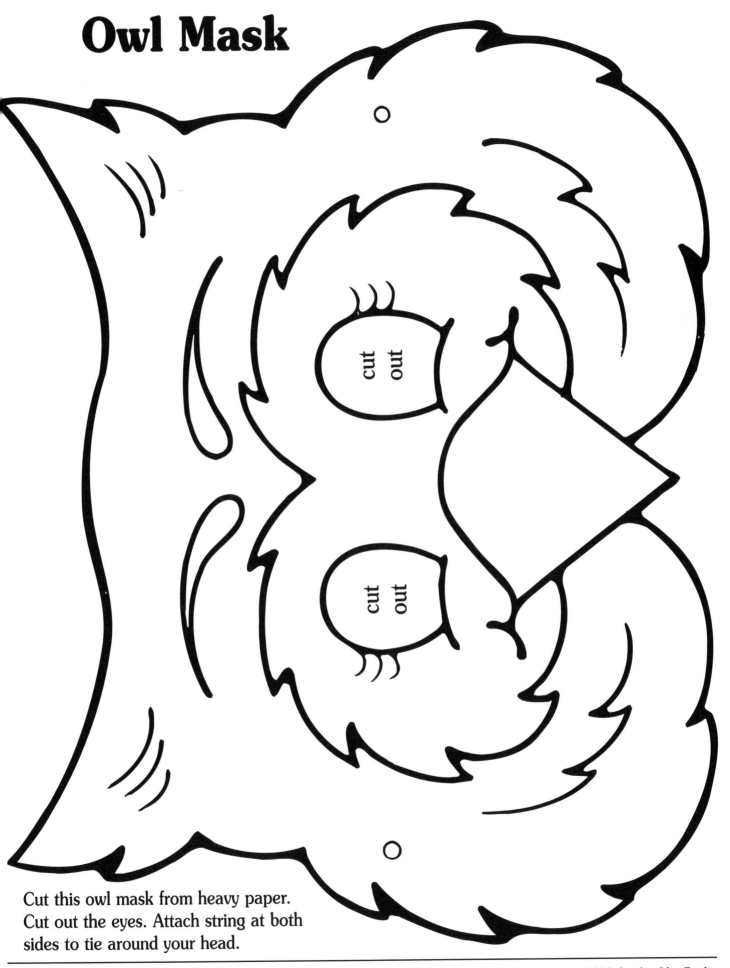

cut out

cut out

Cut this owl mask from heavy paper.
Cut out the eyes. Attach string at both
sides to tie around your head.

Owl Pattern

feet

Cut two wings.

Have each student cut the patterns from brown and orange construction paper. Display "wise" work papers on 9" x 12" sheets of brown paper and assemble the owl

tail

TF1000 October Idea Book

Dinosaurs!

Dinosaur Activities!

Dinosaurs ruled the earth for nearly 100 million years. Discoveries of dinosaur fossils, bones and eggs have helped scientists learn about these fascinating creatures.

All dinosaurs were reptiles. The word "dinosaur" means "terrible lizard." Some of the giant dinosaurs could easily be described in these terms, but many of them were really rather small. Some dinosaurs walked on two feet, while others walked on all four. Some were strictly plant-eaters and others fierce meat-eaters. Some dinosaurs preferred living in or near the water while still others thrived in drier climates. One type of dinosaur, the pterodactyl, even flew like a bird.

Scientists are still puzzled over why the dinosaurs disappeared. Many believe that as the earth slowly changed from a planet of moist warm areas to hot dry ones. A change in climate occurred which depleted the food supply. With plants and water diminishing, the dinosaurs soon died out. Other scientists believe that this change in the earth's climate was caused by a great event, such as a comet or asteroid crashing into the earth. Such an event would have caused a great dust cloud to form in the sky, blocking out the sunlight. With no sunlight, plants soon died and eventually the dinosaurs along with them.

RESEARCH ACTIVITIES

1. Scientists that study fossils are called paleontologists. How do they know where to look for fossils? What type of tools do they use? Draw examples of at least three different fossils a paleontologist might find.

2. Scientists do not really know why the dinosaurs disappeared. Find out what most scientists believe about the prehistoric changes in the earth and what may have caused these changes. What evidence do scientists have? Write a short paper presenting these ideas..

3. On a world map, label the places where dinosaur bones have been discovered. Where have most of the bones been found? Is there a distinct pattern? If so, why? Is there a continent where dinosaur fossils have not yet been found?

4. Make a list of six dinosaurs. Tell whether they were meat-eaters or plant-eaters. List their approximate size. List a special fact about each dinosaur.

   TF1000 October Idea Book

Dinosaur Activities!

PET DINOSAURS

Ask your students to select a type of dinosaur to research. Tell them to record the size, weight, habitat, favorite food and other characteristics.

Now have them write a story in which this dinosaur becomes their personal pet! Have them carefully consider the various problems of owning such an unusual pet. Where would it sleep? What would you feed it? How would the neighbors react? How would the other family pets relate to it? Explain to the children that even though their stories can be fun and entertaining, they must present the actual facts about each dinosaur.

Your students will love reading these stories aloud to their classmates.

DINOSAUR HELPERS

Keep track of your classroom helpers with this "funasaurus" idea! Using cute dinosaur patterns, label each one with the name of a classroom job and add "asaurus" to it. These names could include "Messengerasaurus," "Eraserasaurus," "Leaderasaurus," "Pledgeasaurus," "Petasaurus," etc.

Cut out a colorful paper dinosaur egg for each student and label it with his or her name. When jobs are assigned, place the eggs beneath the appropriate dinosaur.

HOW BIG IS A DINOSAUR?

Children and adults, for that matter, have a hard time imagining large numbers and sizes. Help your students envision the size of a dinosaur with this activity.

Ask the students to choose two or three favorite dinosaurs. Instruct them to find out the estimated height and length of each one. Take a long measuring tape to the playground and have the students mark off each dinosaur's dimensions. Next, ask them to measure the height of the classroom ceiling. Tell them each to divide the ceiling height into the height of the dinosaur to determine how many stories high they might have been. Your students will be amazed to find out how large (and small) some of these ancient creatures were.

DINOSAUR NEWS!

It was once believed that all dinosaurs were slow-moving and cold-blooded. Today, however, many scientists believe that several dinosaurs were warm-blooded and that some could run very fast.

Not long ago, it was also believed that dinosaurs paid little attention to their young. Today it is believed that some dinosaurs were good parents, taking care of their young and protecting them from harm, similar to the way birds take care of their chicks. Some dinosaurs actually lived together in colonies.

Ask older students to research scientists' theories. What new information has been discovered? How did scientists arrive at their conclusions?

Dinosaur Activities!

MAKE A FOSSIL

Have your students create their own "fossils." Ask your pupils to bring some things to fossilize from home, such as leaves, twigs, chicken bones, nut shells, etc. You will also need to collect clean margarine or cottage cheese containers.

The first step is to mix enough water with classroom clay to make "clay slip" (clay that is easily spread). Place about one inch of the slip into the bottom of each container and smooth with a spatula. Now, have the students press the object they are going to fossilize into the clay and then carefully remove it. This will leave an imprint. Let these imprints dry for two or three days.

Real paleontologists often make casts of fossils. Your students can do the same. Spray each imprint with non-stick cooking spray. Spread a thick layer of fresh plaster of Paris over the imprint. When the plaster dries, the students can carefully lift it from the imprint. The plaster mold will show the positive relief of the object they have fossilized.

SIDEWALK FOSSILS

It might not be as rare as you think to find a fossil right outside the classroom door. Small leaves or twigs imprinted into fresh cement or asphalt create "sidewalk fossils!"

Before beginning your fossil hunt, check out the area first to ensure the presence of "fossil" imprints. Explain to your students the definition of a fossil. Take your students on a school yard hunt for fossils. When a fossil is found, have students make a rubbing of the imprint with crayons and paper.

DINOSAUR TASKS

Have your students try some of these dinosaur tasks. Have them research the information in the school library.

• Make a list of eight different dinosaurs. Tell whether they were meat-eaters or plant-eaters. Make a comparative line graph to show which were the smallest and which were the largest.

• Paleontologist are scientists that study fossils. Find out how paleontologists know where to look for fossils. What special tools do they use? How do they prepare and protect the fossils they find? What do they then do with the fossils?

• Why are the dinosaurs extinct? What could have caused them to die out? Write down the three most recognized scientific theories.

• On a world map, mark or label the places where dinosaur bones have been found. Is there a pattern? Is there an area where dinosaur fossils have not been found? Where have most been found? Can you think of a reason why?

Dinosaur Patterns

Use these patterns in a variety of ways. Enlarge them for bulletin board displays or give each child one dinosaur to research.

Tyrannosaurus

Triceratops

Make a matching activity by having students match the dinosaurs' name and description with the corresponding illustration.

Ankylosaurus

Parasaurlophus

Anatosaurus

TF1000 October Idea Book

Brontosaurus

Stegosaurus

TF1000 October Idea Book

Pterodactyl

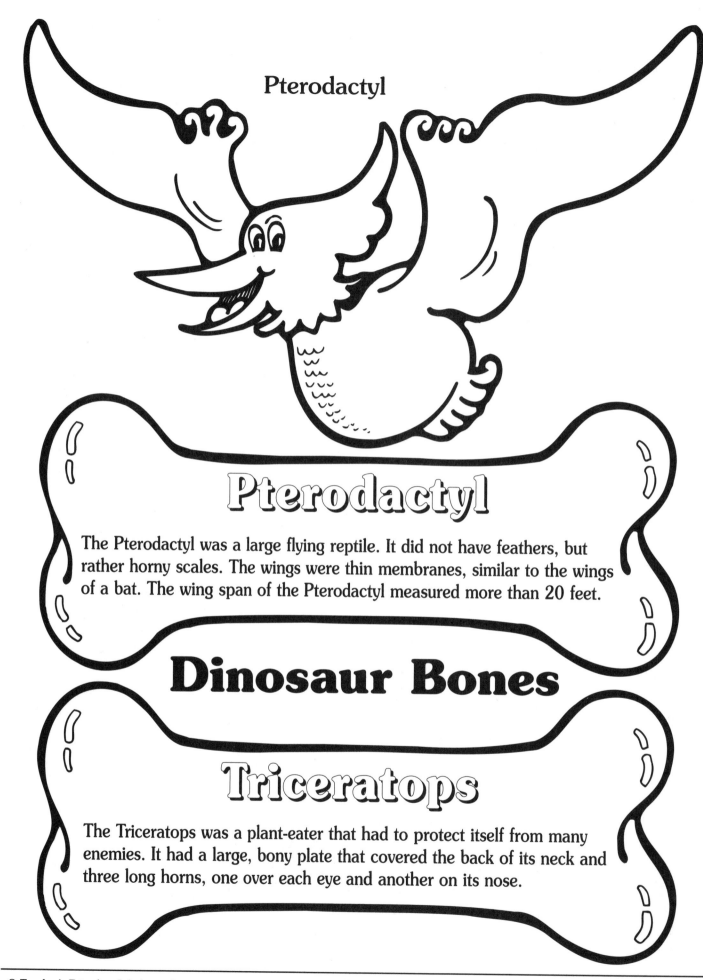

Pterodactyl

The Pterodactyl was a large flying reptile. It did not have feathers, but rather horny scales. The wings were thin membranes, similar to the wings of a bat. The wing span of the Pterodactyl measured more than 20 feet.

Dinosaur Bones

Triceratops

The Triceratops was a plant-eater that had to protect itself from many enemies. It had a large, bony plate that covered the back of its neck and three long horns, one over each eye and another on its nose.

Tyrannosaurus

The "King" of dinosaurs was the Tyrannosaurus. This giant meat-eater measured 45 feet when walking on its two back legs. It also had large, strong jaws and many sharp teeth.

Anatosaurus

The Anatosaurs was a large plant-eating dinosaur. It had a long, wide mouth that resembled a duck bill. These dinosaurs lived near or in the water, where their webbed feet made them good swimmers.

Ankylosaurus

The Ankylosaurus was a plant-eater that was very well protected from its enemies. Its body was almost completely covered with a hard, bony armor. It had long, sharp spikes down its sides and a powerful club-like tail.

Stegosaurus

The Stegosaurus was a medium sized dinosaur measuring about 18 feet long. It was a plant-eater that had a small head and large, bony plates down its back. The spines on its tail helped protect it from its enemies.

Brontosaurus

The giant Brontosaurus was called "Thunder Lizard," apparently because the ground shook as it walked. This plant-eater grew to be 75 feet long and spent most of its time in the water.

Parasaurlophus

The Parasaurlophus had blunt teeth and only ate plants. It used its teeth to strip off twigs and leaves. This unusual animal may have been brightly colored.

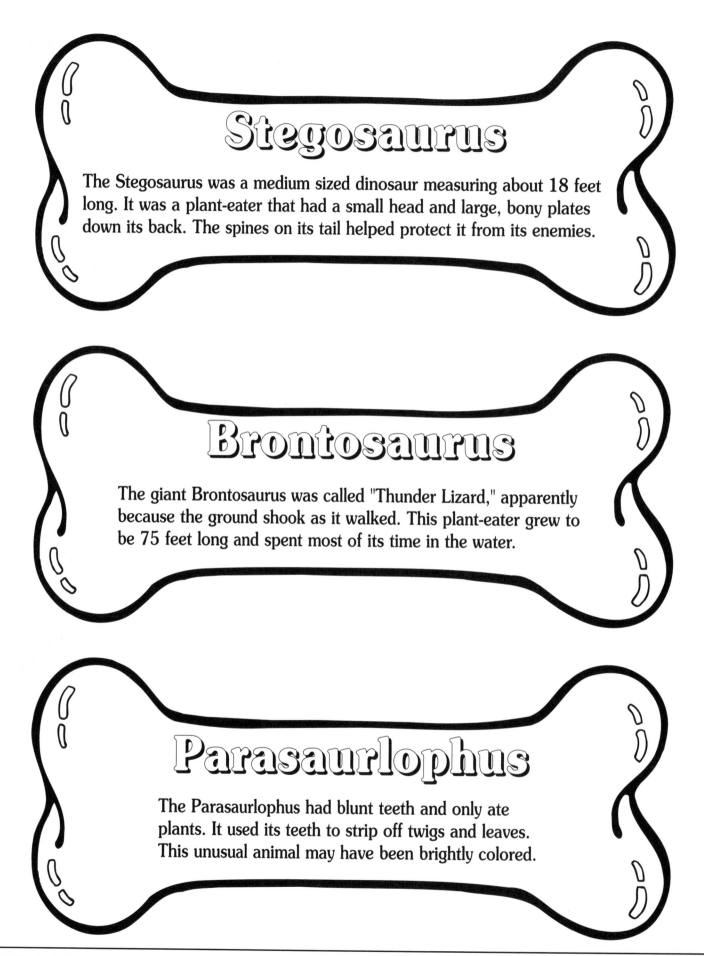

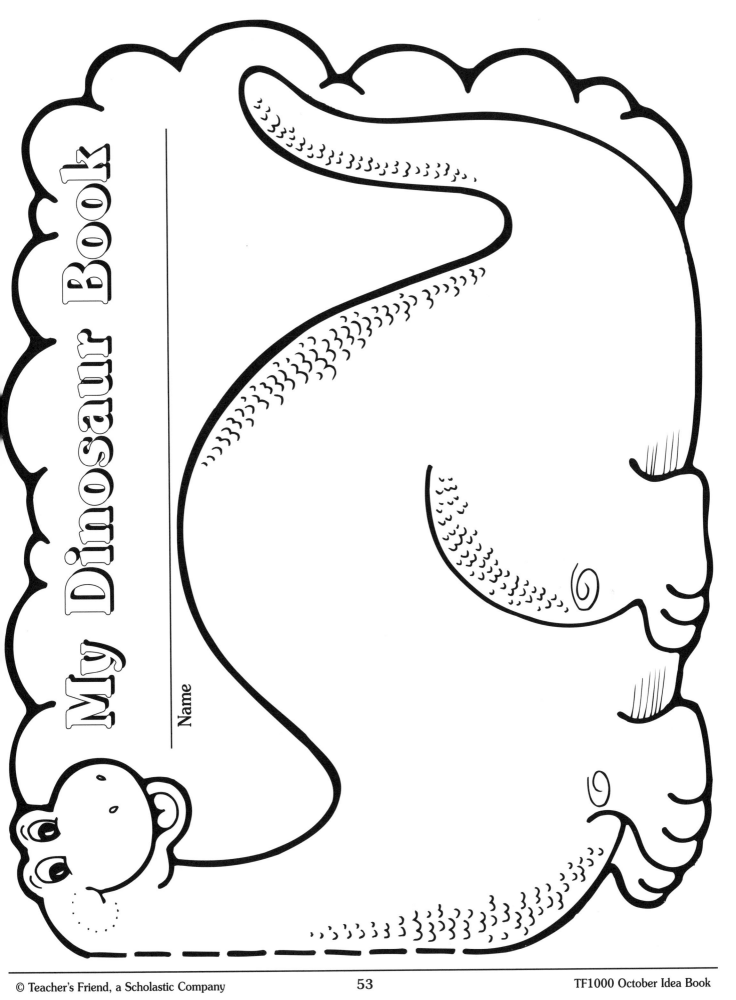

My Dinosaur Book

Name

Creative Writing Page

Write a story about the family that had a pet dinosaur.

_____

- -

_____

_____

- -

_____

_____

- -

_____

_____

- -

_____

_____

- -

_____

_____

- -

_____

_____

- -

_____

_____

- -

_____

Spiders!

Spider Activities!

Spiders can be found just about everywhere! Did you know that spiders are not insects? They are arachnida! That means that they have eight legs instead of six. Most spiders are harmless, but there are a few that can be poisonous. Learn more about spiders by completing some of the activities in this unit.

OBSERVING SPIDERS

A large, clear jar makes a great home for a spider. Place a some long twigs in the jar and add a few drops of water to the bottom. Cover the opening of the jar with gauze secured by a rubber band.

Have each student capture a spider in his or her jar. (Warn the students not to catch the spiders with their bare hands.) Flies and other insects will need to be collected for food. Students should now begin their observations. A magnifying glass might come in handy.

Ask the students to find out the answers to these questions:
What type of spider is it?
How are spiders different from insects?
How are spiderlings born?
What does your spider eat?
How are spiders valuable to humans?
How does a spider spin its web?
Why does it spin a web?

SPIDER WEB BINGO

Use the web pattern contained in this unit, or a simplified web pattern. Give each student a copy of the pattern and ask them to write random numbers in each web section. The teacher randomly calls out numbers from one to one hundred until one pupil marks an entire section of the web leading to the center. That pupil calls out "Bingo!" and wins the game!

CATCH A SPIDER WEB

Catch a spider web with this clever idea:

You will need: black spray paint and white paper or white spray paint and black paper, old newspapers, scissors and a spider web.

After you have found a good spider web (with the spider not home), cover the surrounding ground with newspaper. Lightly spray the web with paint. Make sure you spray both sides of the web.

Carefully bend your paper and place it in the center of the web. The web will stick to the paper because it is still wet with paint. Pull the web away from its anchors very carefully. Allow the web to dry thoroughly. The web can then be displayed on the class board.

SPIDER RESEARCH

Ask your students to answer the following questions:

• What are some of the many reasons that spiders spin silk?

• How do spiders care for their young?

• What are the different types of webs made by spiders?

• How do spiders prepare their prey for food?

• Research spiders that do not build webs. How do they capture their food?

Spider Activities!

STUDENT MADE WEB

Place a large sheet of butcher paper in the center of the floor. Ask students to sit in a circle around the paper. Give one child a large ball of yarn and have him/her tape the end of the yarn to the paper about 3 inches away from the edge. The yarn is then passed to a child on the opposite side of the circle. This child tapes the yarn in place and passes the ball of yarn again. The procedure is repeated until everyone has had a turn.

Lift the paper from the floor and attach it to the class bulletin board. Secure the yarn in place with straight pins.

Students can cut their own spiders from black construction paper and attach them to the web.

DANGEROUS SPIDERS

Over 2,500 varieties of spiders inhabit the United States and Canada. Only two kinds, however, are poisonous. Ask your students to research the following two spiders:

BLACK WIDOW - This spider is found throughout the United States and Southern Canada. The female is the one that bites. You can recognize her by her shiny black or brown color and the red, hour-glass shape on her underside. Black widows are often found in dark, hidden area.

BROWN RECLUSE - This poisonous spider is found only in the Southern and Central United States. Unlike most spiders, it has six eyes rather than eight. It also has a violin-shaped mark on its back. It is usually found under rocks or in other secluded areas.

SPIDER AND FLY

This simple outdoor game will delight your students.

Ask the students to stand in a circle and hold hands. (These students are the web.) Choose one student to be the spider and another student to be the fly.

The fly stands inside the circle and the spider stands outside. The students forming the web move the circle clockwise. When the teacher claps her hands, the circle stops moving and the spider darts inside the web to chase the fly. The fly may run outside the circle. As the spider tries to tag the fly, the students forming the web help the fly by raising and lowering their arms so that the fly can dart in and out. They can also use their arms to block the spider. You may need to set a time limit so that several students have the opportunity to be the spider or fly.

SPIDER RELAY

Young children may like to compete in this spider-related relay race.

Divide the class into several small teams. Instruct students in each team to move in the following manner:

SPIDER WALK - From a sitting position, lean back and place both hands on the ground. Support body weight on all four limbs and "walk" forward.

FLY WALK - While on your knees, flap your arms like wings and hurry to the finish line.

SPIDER EGG - Balance a volley ball on the palm of one hand and rush forward.

Spider Legs

Use this spider pattern to create a cute hanging spider. Cut eight long strips of construction paper per spider. Students can fanfold the strips and staple or glue them to the spider's body.

Spider Pattern

Cut this spider pattern from dark construction paper. Fold the legs inward along the dotted lines. Cut the eyes from white paper and glue in place. Set the spider on a table top or hang it by a string in the classroom.

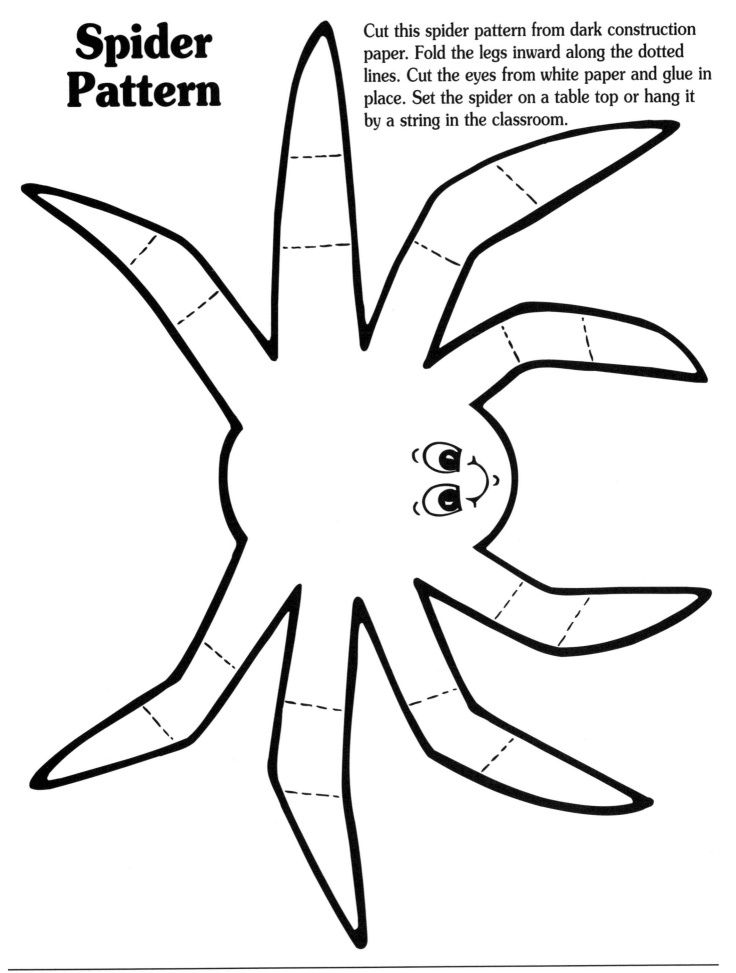

Spider Web Pattern

Use this web pattern to play Spider Web Bingo or have students write spelling words in the web sections.

Spider Crafts!

EGG CARTON SPIDER

Cut the spider legs pattern from black construction paper. Fold the legs along the dotted lines. Cut a section from an egg carton and paint it a desired color. When dry, glue the egg carton section to the top of the spider leg pattern. Make a large spider web on the class bulletin board using white yarn. Let students pin their own spiders to the class web to create a spooky display.

SPIDER WEB "SNOWFLAKE"

Fold a square piece of white paper in half and then again in thirds. Square off each section, as shown, so that you now have a hexagon shape. Cut away sections, alternating from side to side. Carefully open the web. Children can display their "egg carton spiders" along with their spider web "snowflakes."

My Spider Report

_____

- - - - - - - - - - - - - - - - - -

Spider Name

```
┌─────────────────────────────┐
│                             │
│                             │
│                             │
│                             │
│                             │
│                             │
└─────────────────────────────┘
```
Picture of my Spider

```
┌─────────────────────────────┐
│                             │
│                             │
│                             │
│                             │
│                             │
│                             │
│                             │
└─────────────────────────────┘
```
Picture of the Web

This spider is....

☐ **poisonous**

☐ **non-poisonous**

This spider can be found _____

_____

_____

It eats _____

_____

_____

This spider has....

☐ **legs**

☐ **eyes**

Some interesting facts about my spider! _____

_____

_____

_____

_____

_____

Skeletons!

No Bones About It!

No Bones About It!

With Halloween fast approaching, students will be fascinated with and eager to learn about skeletons.

Our bodies contain 206 skeletal bones. Without our skeletons, we would be a shapeless mass, much like a jellyfish. While most of our bones give our bodies structure and strength, many bones also serve another important purpose. These bones carefully protect our sensitive organs. For example, the skull protects our brain, while our rib cage and breast bone protect our lungs and heart.

Our skeletal bones are very much alive. Each bone is actually hollow and contains a soft material inside known as marrow. Marrow makes our bones lighter and easier to move, yet strong enough to support our bodies.

This rigid skeleton also does a remarkable thing: It grows! Our bodies absorb minerals such as calcium, from the foods we eat and turns these minerals into the hard bones that make up our skeletons.

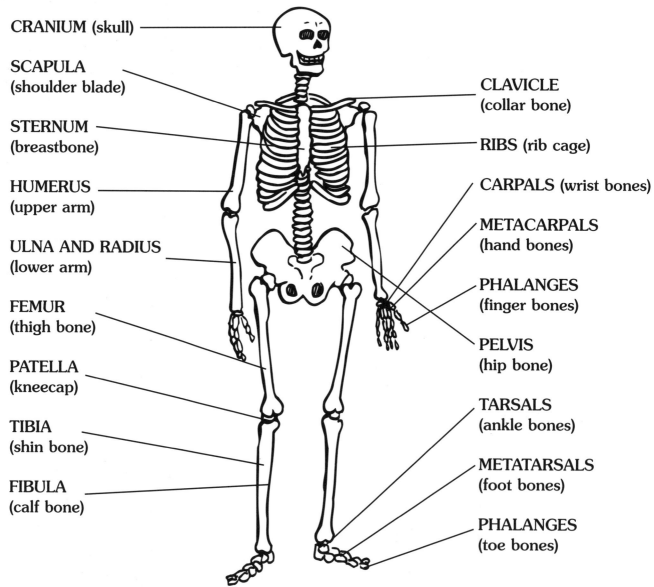

CRANIUM (skull)

SCAPULA
(shoulder blade)

STERNUM
(breastbone)

HUMERUS
(upper arm)

ULNA AND RADIUS
(lower arm)

FEMUR
(thigh bone)

PATELLA
(kneecap)

TIBIA
(shin bone)

FIBULA
(calf bone)

CLAVICLE
(collar bone)

RIBS (rib cage)

CARPALS (wrist bones)

METACARPALS
(hand bones)

PHALANGES
(finger bones)

PELVIS
(hip bone)

TARSALS
(ankle bones)

METATARSALS
(foot bones)

PHALANGES
(toe bones)

Skeleton Match!

After your students have become familiar with the common and proper names for the major bones, play a "Simple Simon" type of game. "Mr. Skeleton says.....touch your cranium."

ACTIVITY 1

MATCH THE COMMON NAMES OF BONES
WITH THEIR PROPER NAMES.

CRANIUM	Collar Bone
FIBULA	Kneecap
PATELLA	Hand and Foot Bones
ULNA AND RADIUS	Shoulder Blade
SCAPULA	Calf Bone
STERNUM	Thigh Bone
HUMERUS	Breastbone
FEMUR	Shin Bone
TIBIA	Finger and Toe Bones
CLAVICLE	Hip Bone
PELVIS	Ankle Bones
METACARPALS/METATARSALS	Skull
PHALANGES	Wrist Bones
CARPALS	Upper Arm Bone
TARSALS	Lower Arm Bones

TF1000 October Idea Book

Mr. Skeleton

Display the Mr. Skeleton pattern on the classroom bulletin board and list names of important bones on strips of paper. Students will enjoy researching these bones and labeling the various areas of the skeleton.

Make enough copies of Mr. Skeleton for everyone in the class. Children will love assembling their own skeletons with brass fasteners and displaying them at home, on Halloween.

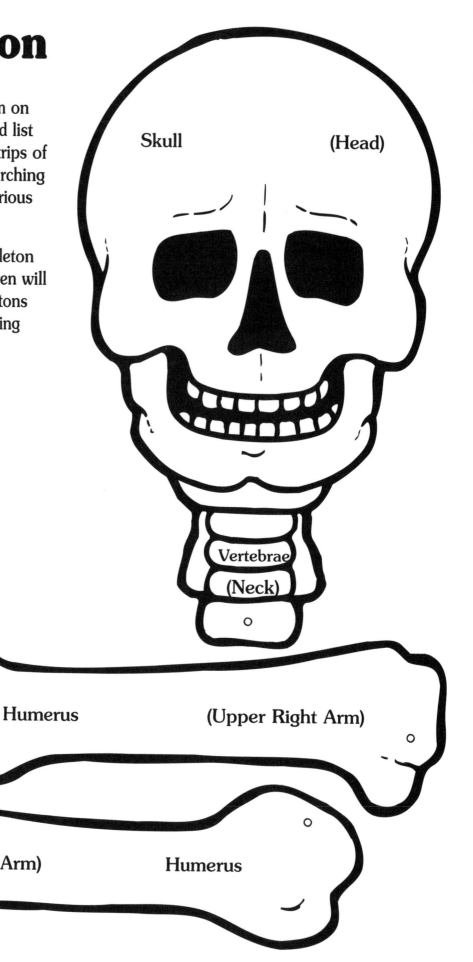

Skull   (Head)

Vertebrae

(Neck)

Humerus   (Upper Right Arm)

(Upper Left Arm)   Humerus

TF1000 October Idea Book

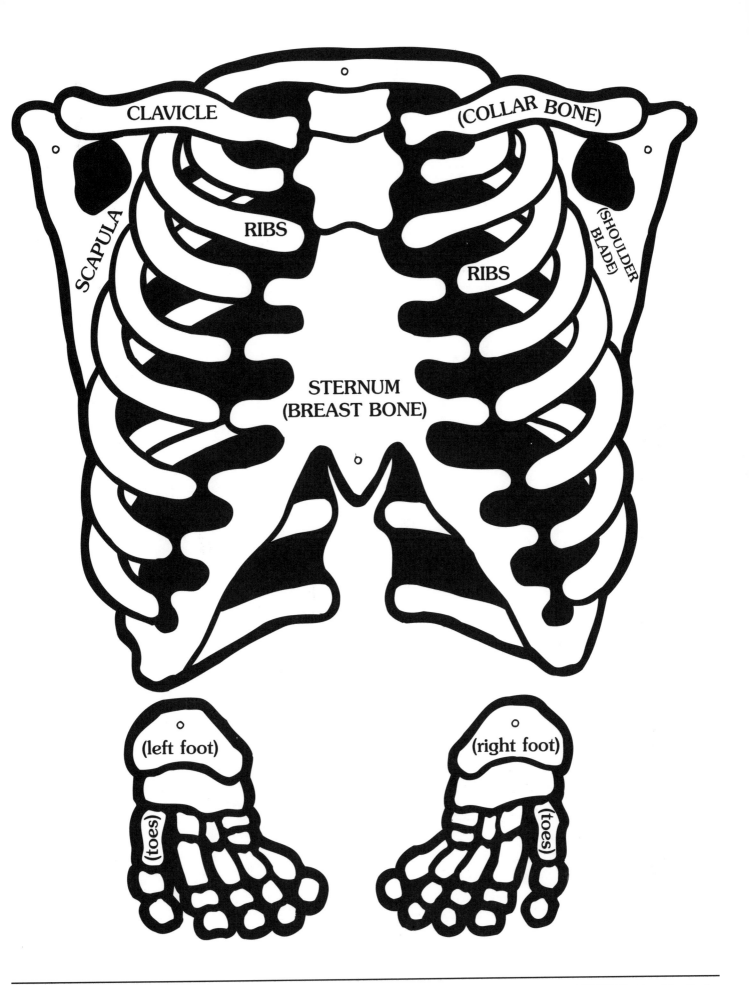

CLAVICLE

(COLLAR BONE)

SCAPULA

RIBS

(SHOULDER BLADE)

RIBS

STERNUM
(BREAST BONE)

(left foot)

(right foot)

(toes)

(toes)

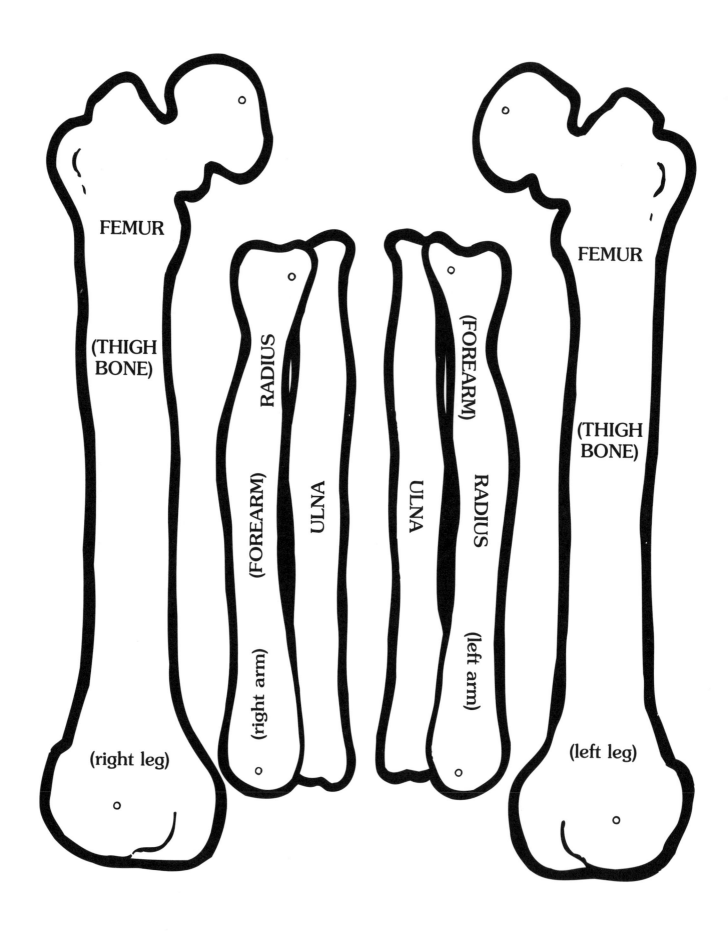

FEMUR

(THIGH BONE)

(right leg)

RADIUS

(FOREARM)

ULNA

(right arm)

(FOREARM)

ULNA

RADIUS

(left arm)

FEMUR

(THIGH BONE)

(left leg)

68

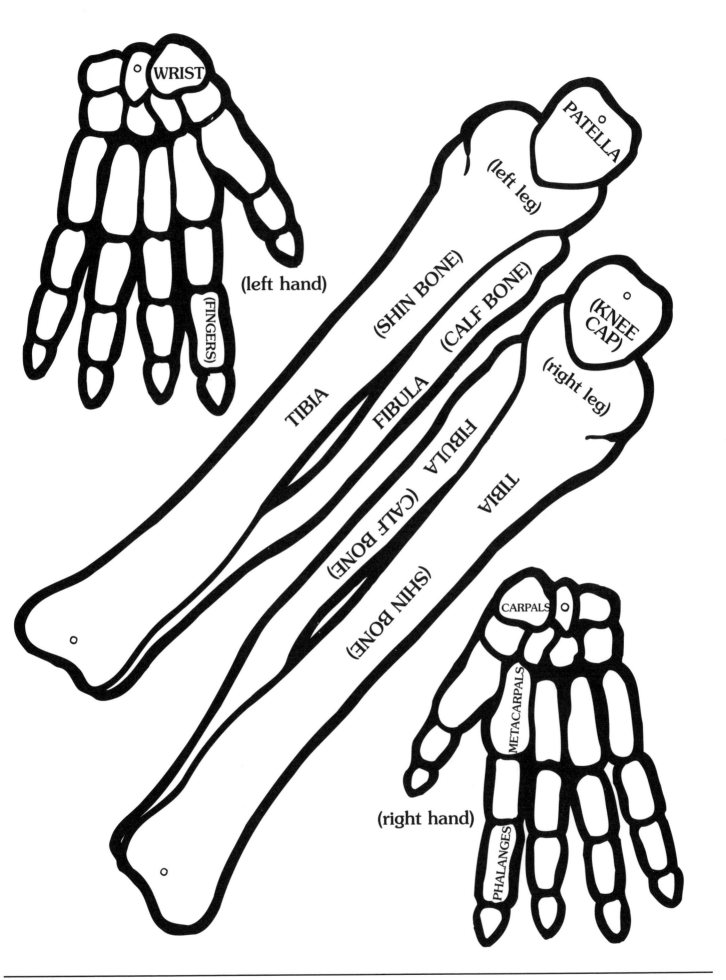

WRIST

(left hand)

(FINGERS)

PATELLA

(left leg)

(SHIN BONE)

(CALF BONE)

TIBIA

FIBULA

(KNEE CAP)

(right leg)

FIBULA

(CALF BONE)

TIBIA

(SHIN BONE)

CARPALS

METACARPALS

(right hand)

PHALANGES

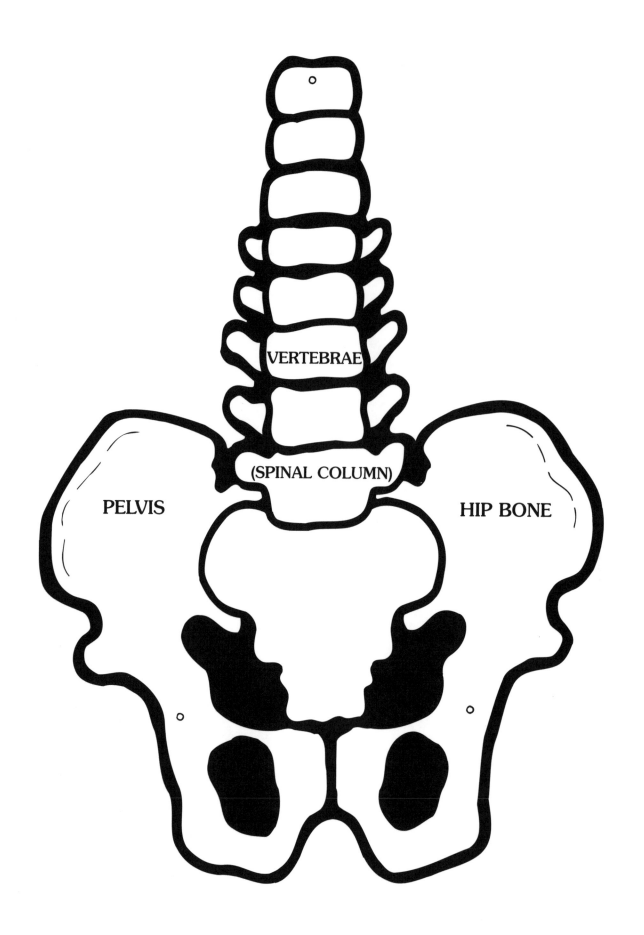

VERTEBRAE

(SPINAL COLUMN)

PELVIS

HIP BONE

TF1000 October Idea Book

Skeleton Activities!

LIFE-SIZED SKELETONS

Motivate your students into learning about the human body with a life-sized skeleton!

Have students trace around each other's bodies on large sheets of butcher paper and cut them out. Give the children the Mr. Skeleton patterns to cut out and paste on top of their body shapes. (The Mr. Skeleton patterns contained in this unit are just the right size for most kindergartners. Enlarge the patterns for older students.) The skeletons can be displayed on the class board as an informative but fun way to learn the bones of the body.

FLASHLIGHT X-RAY

After a discussion about the human skeleton, have your students experience viewing their own bones with this intriguing activity.

Darken the room and ask each child to take a turn holding the palm of their hand over a flashlight. If they look carefully, the children will be able to see the bones and joints connecting the fingers. Students can draw pictures of what they see.

DID YOU KNOW...

The largest bone in the body is the thigh bone, or *femur*. It measures about 20 inches long in a person six feet tall. The smallest bone in the body is the stirrup bone. It is found in the ear and is only one-tenth of an inch long.

BODY MATH

When a baby is born, he has 300 bones in his body. As an adult, he will have only 206. The reason he has fewer is that many of the bones will fuse together as he grows.

Using the following count of bones in the body, ask your student to calculate a variety of math problems.

32 bones in each arm
31 bones in each leg
29 bones in the skull
26 bones in the spine
25 bones in the chest

Here are some other body statistics that can be used for math word problems and at the same time provide knowledge of the human body.

The human body contains about 8 pints of blood.

About 400 gallons of blood flows through your kidneys each day.

The small intestine is 20 feet long and the large intestine is 5 feet long.

The body is made up of about 70% water, or about 3/4 of your body weight.

Your heart beats about 100,000 times a day.

You blink your eyes about 20,000 times a day.

Skull Puppet

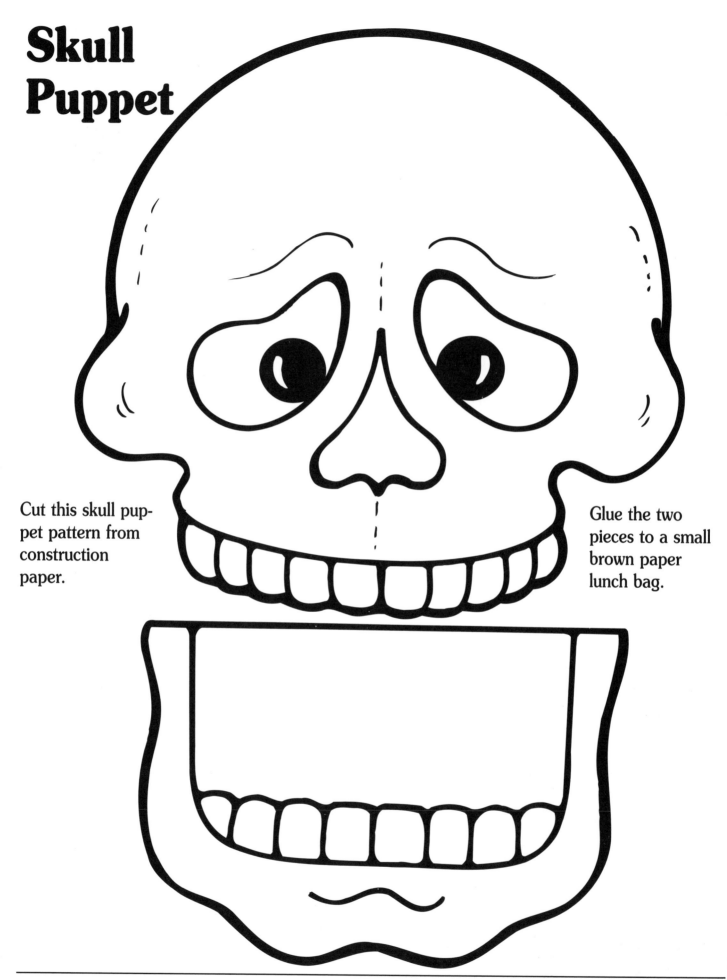

Cut this skull puppet pattern from construction paper.

Glue the two pieces to a small brown paper lunch bag.

Masks!

Masks Around the World!

Throughout the history of the world, masks have played an important role in celebrations, death ceremonies and theatrical plays. Masks can cover the entire face or only part of the face. They can be made from a variety of materials, including wood, paper and gold.

EGYPT

The Egyptians made death masks by making wax impressions of the deceased face. These masks were covered with sheets of gold and were believed to protect the deceased from evil spirits.

Show the class pictures of King Tutankhamen's treasures, including his death mask. Students might like to make life-sized sculptures of their own faces from clay. Later, papier-mache masks can be made over the face sculptures. When dry, they can spray-paint the masks gold and display them on a bulletin board entitled "Our Egyptian Masks."

AFRICA

Masks are very important in African ceremonies. An African dancer might wear a beautiful mask of a spirit or animal. Masks are often believed to contain great powers and are handled with respect. Members of certain African tribes believe that a person can stop being him or herself, for a short time, when a mask or costume is used as a disguise.

Children might like to make an animal paper-bag mask. Older students could research the African cultures and find pictures of various ceremonial masks.

Masks Around the World!

NORTH AMERICA

The Indian tribes of North America use masks in many ceremonies and rituals. The Iroquois people carve masks from living trees, which keep the masks "alive" and preserve their magical powers. The masks are painted red if cut in the morning and black if cut later in the day. These "false faces" are carefully carved with the eyes rimmed in metal that glow in the light of the campfire. Horse-tail hair is used to make wigs.

Have children draw pictures of masks that they think Iroquois warriors might make. Tell them to color the masks with bright colors and write brief descriptions of their masks.

MEXICO AND SOUTH AMERICA

The ancient people of Mexico and South America made beautiful relief masks from thin sheets of gold. These early craftsmen used gold in their designs because it was easy to work with and so very plentiful. These masks were usually used to tell stories and for entertainment.

Buy several sheets of copper or brass foil from local craft stores. (Heavy-duty aluminum foil also works well.) Using dull pencils to draw designs, students can simulate the artwork done by Latin-American craftsmen.

GREECE

Early Greeks wore animal masks to worship their gods. Later, this developed into theatrical use in which actors wore masks on stage. One person could play several roles by simply changing masks. The masks often contained small megaphones to help the audience hear the actor. Greek theatrical masks usually fell into two categories, tragedy or comedy.

Have students act out short skits using masks. They might like to create original plays or use familiar stories, such as fairy tales or nursery rhymes.

Masks Around the World!

ALASKA

Inuits of Alaska carve ceremonial masks from driftwood that is washed in by the sea. The men of the tribe often make these masks to represent spirits that are said to give them good luck in fishing and hunting. Eagle feathers, seal skin and animal fur are usually used as decoration. Inuits wear the masks while performing ceremonial dances.

The Inuit women carve small masks that fit easily on their fingers. During the ceremonial dance, they wave their hands and finger masks to the rhythm of the music. Every Inuit dance tells a story. The dancer often makes up the story as the dance continues.

INUIT FINGER MASK

Make this Inuit Finger Mask from construction paper. Cut out and color it as you wish. Cut holes for your fingers. Fringe may be cut and pasted along the outside edge.

Mexican Mask

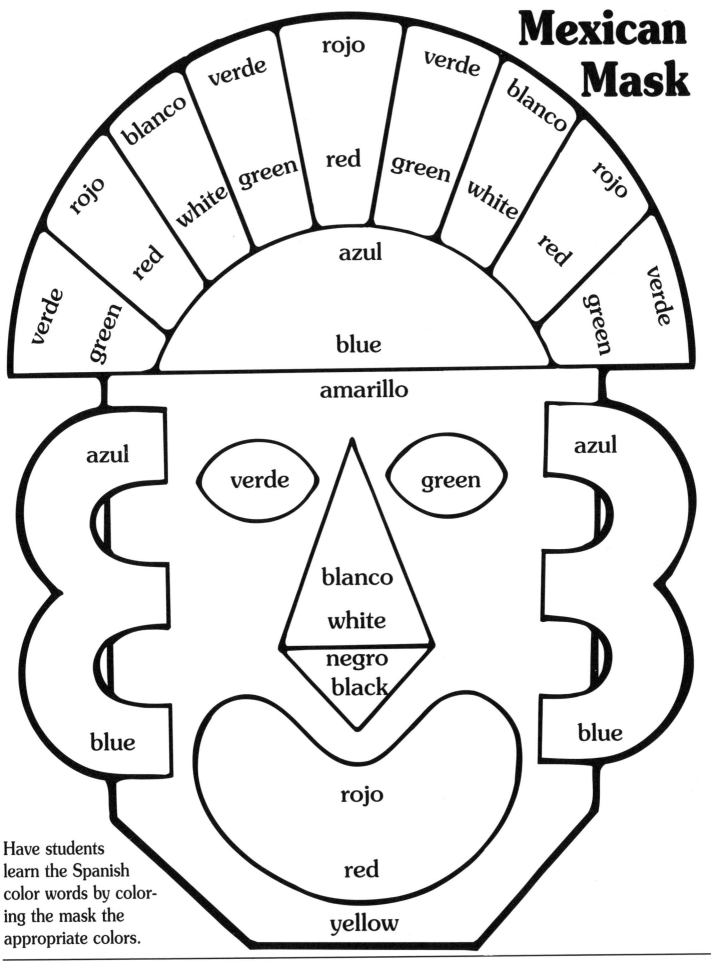

Have students learn the Spanish color words by coloring the mask the appropriate colors.

Mask Patterns

Cut the mask patterns from construction paper and have children create a variety of different masks for any costume.

Children will love using their imaginations to create faces and characters. Let them add pipe cleaner whiskers, glitter, cotton and sequins for that extra-special look.

Cat and Bunny Nose

Cat Ears

Mask Pattern

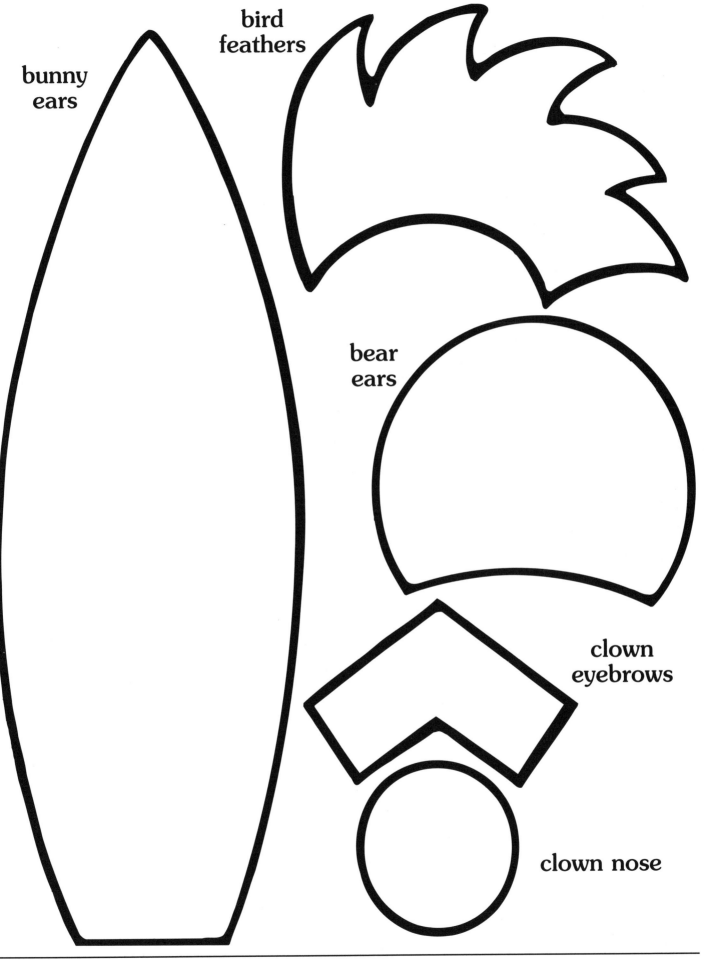

bunny
ears

bird
feathers

bear
ears

clown
eyebrows

clown nose

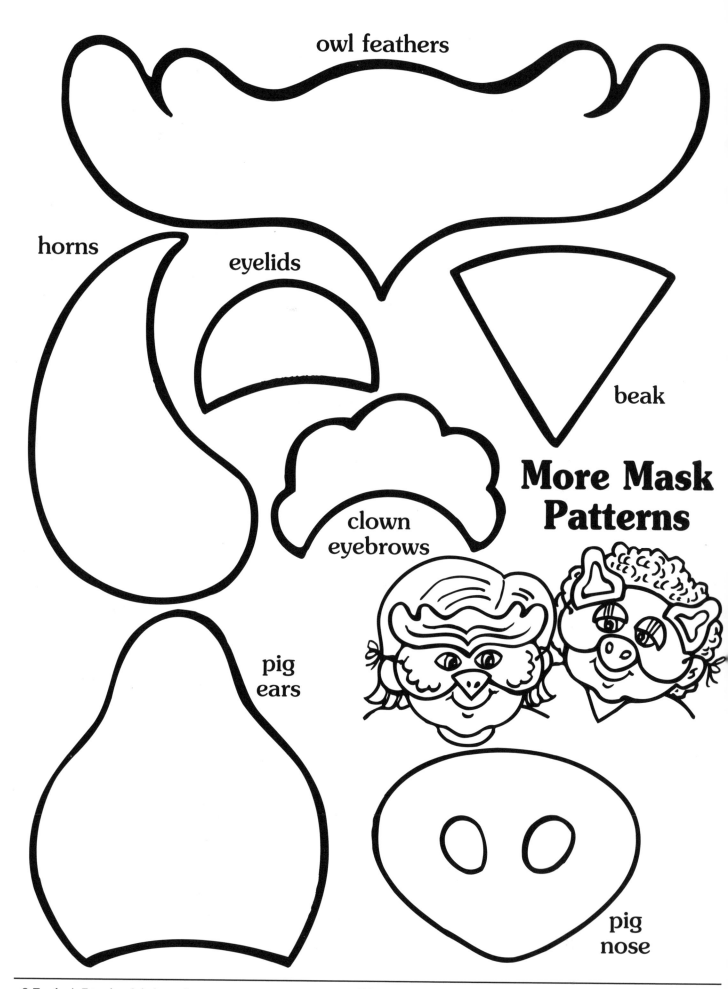

owl feathers

horns

eyelids

beak

clown eyebrows

More Mask Patterns

pig ears

pig nose

glamour eyes

dog ears

nose and mustache

dog or bear nose

eyebrows

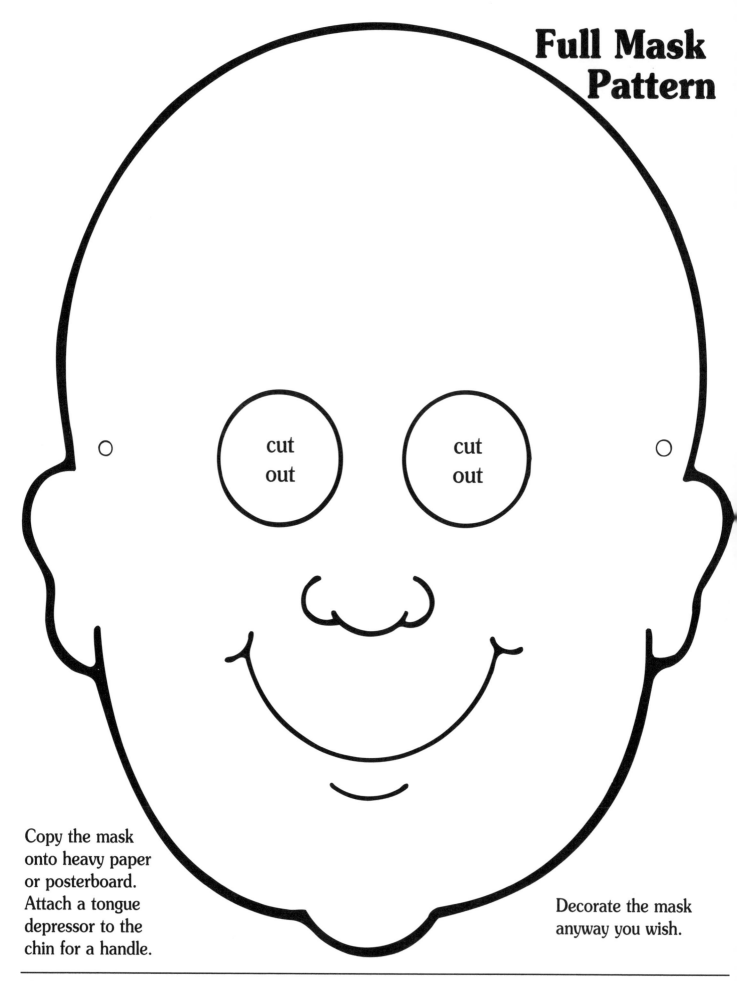

Full Mask Pattern

cut out

cut out

Copy the mask onto heavy paper or posterboard. Attach a tongue depressor to the chin for a handle.

Decorate the mask anyway you wish.

TF1000 October Idea Book

Columbus Day!

On August 3, 1492, Christopher Columbus set sail from Spain in search of the East Indies. Columbus sailed west across the then uncharted Atlantic Ocean. Eighty-eight men made up the crews of the "Niña," "Pinta," and "Santa Maria."

The journey was a long and difficult one. The crews became terrified at their failure to find land and threatened mutiny. Before dawn on October 12, 1492, the ships landed on an island in the Bahamas. With island natives looking on, Columbus reverently claimed the land for Spain and called it "San Salvador." He was disappointed not to find the wealthy cities and grand civilizations that had been speculated. Instead, he found a culture very different from the Europeans.

Columbus had discovered what he called the New World, and for this he was honored by King Ferdinand and Queen Isabella of Spain. The land Columbus discovered soon became known as "America," after Amerigo Vespucci, who later explored the mainland for Portugal. One thing, however, is certain: Christopher Columbus was a man of vision and courage. He conquered the Atlantic Ocean and opened the New World for others to follow.

COLUMBUS WORD FIND

ACTIVITY 2

FIND THESE WORDS IN THE PUZZLE BELOW:
COLUMBUS, NIÑA, PINTA, SANTA MARIA, SPAIN, SAN SALVADOR, NEW WORLD, AMERICA, KING FERDINAND, QUEEN ISABELLA

```
D V B H Y U J K O L M N H G V B H F R T Y
C O L U M B U S S E R T G Y H U J K I L P
W E R T G Y H P D C V B Q S E R T Y U I P
Z C V F G T H A S W R T U F G H Y U J M N
C F G R T B N I F R T Y E D R Y H J P S Q
S C V B G F D N R T Y H E C O L K I I N G
A M E T Y F E B C D R W N Q X C V T N H U
N E S A N T A M A R I A I F V B G T T D R
S W E T Y G H U I J K Y S D R T Y E A V F
B G T Y U J H F G T V B A M E R I C A T U
W E R T G D V F H F T R B W T Y U P I B N
Q U E F T G H K I N G F E R D I N A N D R
D C V G H B G F V F D S L S R T G Y T R E
D N E W W O R L D F T E L F R T Y G F R E
F B V C D S A N S A L V A D O R F T Y H U
S D F G T Y H U J N B V C X Z D R T G D R
S R V B N M K J G F D N I Ñ A S E F Y H O
```

Discovery Map!

The discovery made by Christopher Columbus changed the history of the world. Write a story using one of these ideas:

- You are Christopher Columbus and about to set sail for the New World.

- You are a crew member of the "Santa Maria."

- You are a native that has just seen three strange ships approaching your island.

- You are Isabella I, Queen of Spain.

Niña, Pinta and......

Color and cut out Columbus' three ships from construction paper.

Fan-fold a large sheet of blue construction paper. Cut three slits in the folds, one behind the other. Slide the ships into the openings and make them stand upright.

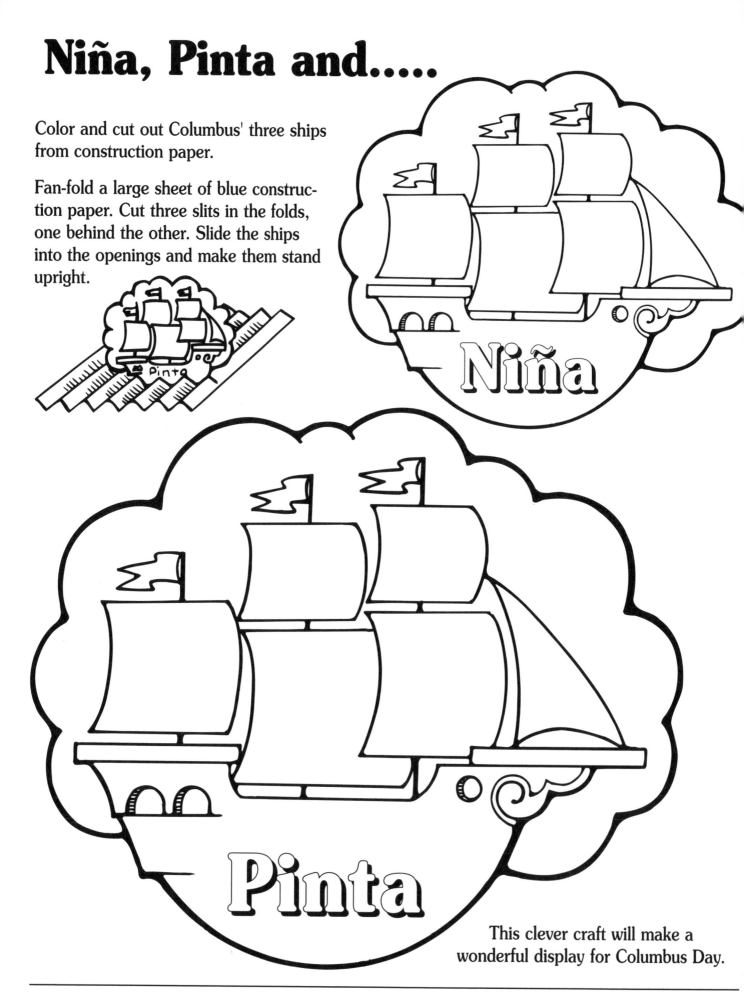

This clever craft will make a wonderful display for Columbus Day.

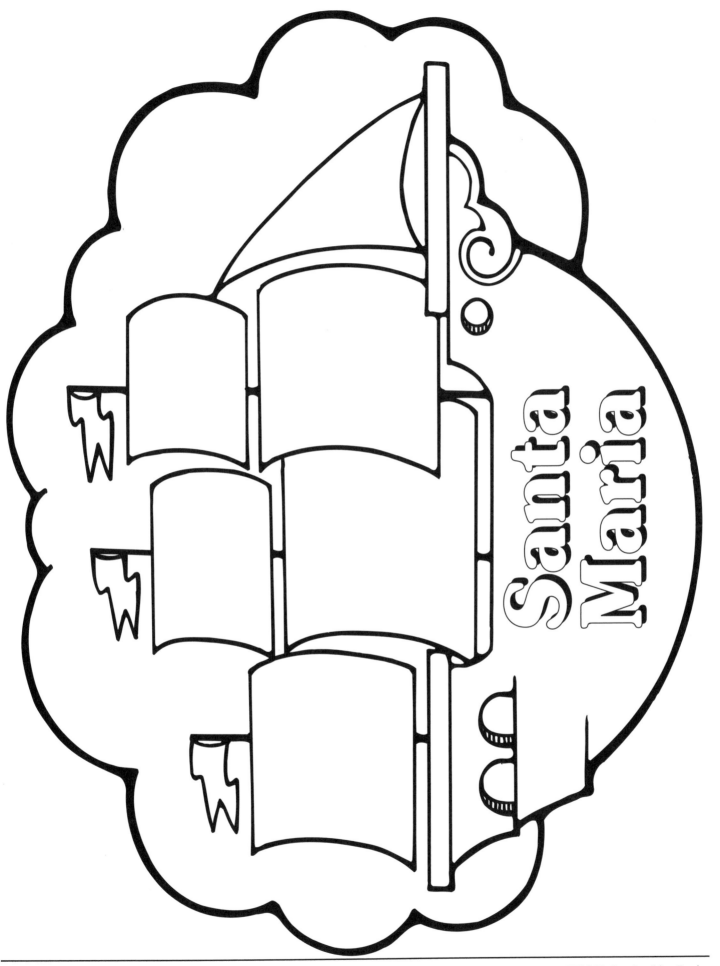

Santa Maria

Columbus Hat

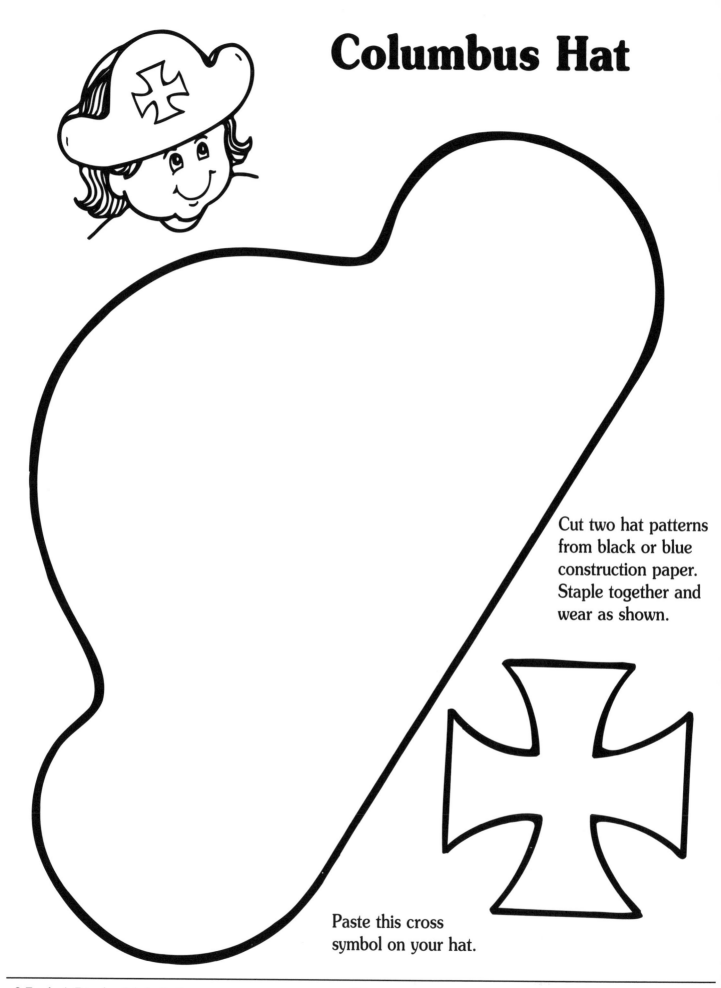

Cut two hat patterns from black or blue construction paper. Staple together and wear as shown.

Paste this cross symbol on your hat.

TF1000 October Idea Book

Columbus Puppet

Color and cut these pattern pieces. Paste them to a small lunch bag.

Have students role-play the discovery made by Columbus using the puppets.

TF1000 October Idea Book

Sailors Wanted!

Christopher Columbus, as commissioned by Queen Isabella of Spain, will set sail for the New World on August 3, 1492. Write the reasons why you should be hired for the voyage.

_____

_____

_____

_____

_____

_____

_____

_____

_____

_____

_____

_____

_____

_____

_____

_____

_____

Fire Safety Activities!

1. Ask students to find newspaper accounts of recent fires. Read them to the class and discuss how they could have been prevented.

2. Suggest that students question friends and family members to learn about their experiences with fire. Have the children tell the class their findings and let the students participate in deciding what should have been done in the same circumstances.

3. Ask students to research fire safety pertaining to a particular holiday. Students might like to choose the 4th of July, with fireworks, Christmas, with lights and candles, or Halloween, with it's jack-o-lanterns.

4. Draw a map of your class's fire drill route on the chalk board. Tell the children about the importance of following the rules and the need to be speedy during a fire emergency.

5. Instruct students on what to do if their clothing catches fire. Select one child to demonstrate to the class how to roll on the floor. Another child can pretend to smother the flames with a blanket. Ask students to discuss how this type of fire emergency could be prevented.

6. Arrange for a firefighter to visit your class. Before his or her visit, have students list questions that they wish to ask.

7. Have students role-play an emergency in which a neighbor's house is burning. Students can use a toy telephone to practice dialing the emergency number and giving the information needed by the fire department.

Create an informative bulletin board by enlarging a large telephone onto poster board. Emergency numbers should be listed for the children's information.

Students might like to find pictures of possible fire dangers and display them on the board with various fire safety guidelines.

Firefighter's Hat and Badge

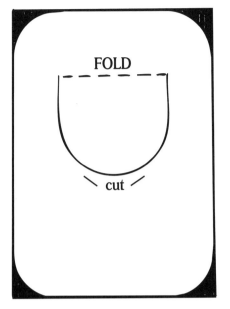

FOLD

cut

Enlarge this simple hat pattern onto 12" x 18" red construction paper. Cut out and fold where indicated.

Ask students to glue a yellow "Official Fire Safety Inspector" badge to the center of the hat.

OFFICIAL FIRE SAFETY INSPECTOR

Name

FIRE SAFETY CERTIFICATE

_____
Name

has demonstrated
Fire Safety!

_____

_____

_____   _____
Teacher   Date

Fire Safety Plan!

MY FAMILY'S ESCAPE PLAN

_____

Family Name

_____

Address

Here is a drawing of my family's home showing our escape plan.

Fire Safety Escape Map

IN CASE OF FIRE, FOLLOW THESE DIRECTIONS.

1. If fire breaks out, alert others by shouting "FIRE!" or by sounding an alarm.

2. If you smell smoke, drop down and crawl to an exit.

3. Touch closed doors first. Open only if they are not hot!

4. If your clothes catch fire, do not run! Stop, Drop and Roll!

5. Follow the best escape route as quickly as possible.

6. Meet other family members at the designated area.

7. Call <u>911</u> from a neighbor's house.

8. Do not go back into the house!

My Fire Safety Check List

AROUND THE HOUSE

YES   **NO**

☐ ☐ Are all electrical cords in good condition?

☐ ☐ Are smoke detectors in place, particularly near the bedrooms? Do they work?

☐ ☐ Are electrical outlets overloaded with too many cords?

☐ ☐ Does your family have at least one fire extinguisher? Does everyone know where it is and how to use it?

☐ ☐ Are portable heaters kept away from drapes, furniture, flammable materials and young children?

☐ ☐ Does the fireplace have a tight-fitting screen or glass door?

☐ ☐ If there are smokers in the family, are they careful never to smoke in bed?

☐ ☐ Are newspapers, trash, and flammable liquids kept away from furnaces and water heaters?

☐ ☐ Is gasoline kept tightly capped in a metal container?

☐ ☐ Are oily rags, trash and sawdust kept cleaned up?

☐ ☐ Are foods always supervised during cooking?

☐ ☐ Are pot handles turned inward on the stove, away from small children?

☐ ☐ Are curtains, towels and paper kept away from the stove?

☐ ☐ Do those who cook know not to wear loose, flowing clothing near the stove?

☐ ☐ Are leaves, dried grass, weeds and other trash kept away from the house and cleaned up quickly?

☐ ☐ If you have a gasoline lawnmower, do the persons using it know how to safely use the gasoline?

☐ ☐ During family barbeques, does the person doing the cooking know never to squirt lighter fluid on hot coals?

Firefighter

Let each student make his or her own firefighter upon which to display a fire safety report or creative writing page.

FIRE DEPT.
7

Or, make a larger firefighter to display fire safety rules.

FIRE SAFETY!

Name

HOT TOPIC!

FIRE DRILL RULES

ROOM # _____

_____
_____
_____
_____
_____
_____
_____
_____
_____

Fire Safety!

FIRE SAFETY BULLETIN BOARD

Create this fire safety bulletin board by dividing the class into two groups. Assign one group to list the "Do's" of fire prevention and the other group the "Don'ts." Examples might include "DO check that all smoke detectors are in working order!" or "DON'T play with matches!"

Give students yellow or red copies of the "Hot Topic" flame page contained in this unit and instruct them to write their fire prevention wisdom on the flames. Display the flames on a special fire prevention bulletin board along with a large Fire Fighter character announcing the good fire fighting habits learned by your students!

EMERGENCY PHONE NUMBERS

Instruct students to fill out the emergency numbers used by their families and post these numbers near the phone at home, in case of an emergency.

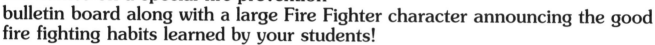

EMERGENCY NUMBERS

911 Police

911 Fire Dept.

911 Ambulance

911 Poison Control

_____ Mom's Work

_____ Dad's Work

_____

Halloween!

Halloween - October 31

No one knows exactly when Halloween was first celebrated. It is believed that the ancient Druids of England were the first to recognize this special day. The Druids observed their New Year's Day on November 1st. The night before, October 31st, was considered their New Year's Eve. They believed that on this night, the lord of the dead called forth the evil spirits to visit the earth. Druids lit great fires on this night to scare them away. They also dressed as ghosts and goblins in hopes of escaping the night unharmed.

Eventually, this celebration became the Christian holiday of All Hallow's Day. The Christians spent this day honoring the saints of the Church. The night before, on All Hallow's Eve (or Halloween) people dressed in masks and costumes meant to represent the saints. It was their duty to lead the spirits of the dead out of town before the next day's celebrations.

After the Romans conquered Britain, harvest festivals became a part of the Halloween celebrations. In Scotland, farmers carried torches through fields in hopes of a good crop for the next yea,.and also to frighten away witches and ghosts that might be hiding in orchards and pastures. People in Ireland hollowed out and carved potatoes and turnips which were lit from inside by candles and used to scare away evil spirits.

Halloween has changed through the years. Next to Christmas, Halloween is the favorite holiday of many children. It is a time to dress up, pretend and explore the neighborhood in search of treats.

When writing spooky Halloween stories, have students try using some of these colorful words in place of common Halloween words, witch, ghost, scary, and dark.

WITCH:
- hag
- sorceress
- soothsayer
- siren
- demon
- warlock

GHOST:
- ghoul
- phantom
- spirit
- spook
- fiend
- poltergeist

SCARY:
- frightful
- spooky
- awesome
- grim
- horrifying
- ghastly
- terrifying
- fiendish

DARK:
- vague
- cloudy
- hazy
- shadow
- foggy
- dim
- gloomy

Halloween Poem!

H
A
L
L
O
W
E
E
N

Using the letters
H-A-L-L-O-W-E-E-N,
write a spooky poem
or list scary vocabu-
lary words.

TF1000 October Idea Book

Halloween
Word Find

```
W P U M P K I N K S D F G H Y T G R Y
E S F T Y U H J K W Y R V H I K O L P
W P T Y H A L L O W E E N T U N J H U
Q O S K E L E T O N M X D R T Y H J G
E O F G T Y H J U K A W E T Y U I O H
J K R C S W E R T H S Y O R A N G E O
F Y E D F R T G B V K R E T G H Y J S
O C T O B E R G T Y H H J M N I U O T
W A C F T Y U I J H N M K L P O N B D
U N S R C O S T U M E V G Y H N M J U
Z D T R I C K O R T R E A T V G Y N H
M Y X C V G H Y J K R F B N B W E T R
S D R F B H G T R D C X A W E Q X V B
S E R T Y U J N H B F R T S W E V B N
M A S D R F G T D V G R S C V B N L Q
A C V F T H N J U T G N B F E R T A V
J A C K O L A N T E R N C F R W T C E
J A W C V B H Y U N M K L H U Y R K W
Q C B G T R F E S C F T H W I T C H M
```

ACTIVITY 3

FIND THESE HIDDEN WORDS: CANDY, COSTUME, MASK, JACK O' LANTERN, ORANGE, BLACK, SKELETON, SPOOKY, TRICK OR TREAT, BATS, GHOST, WITCH, PUMPKIN, HALLOWEEN, OCTOBER.

WRITE A POEM OR STORY USING AS MANY OF THE WORDS AS POSSIBLE!

_____

_____

_____

_____

Cut the two pumpkin pieces and the ghost from construction paper. Assemble with a brass fastener.

Pumpkin 'n Ghost

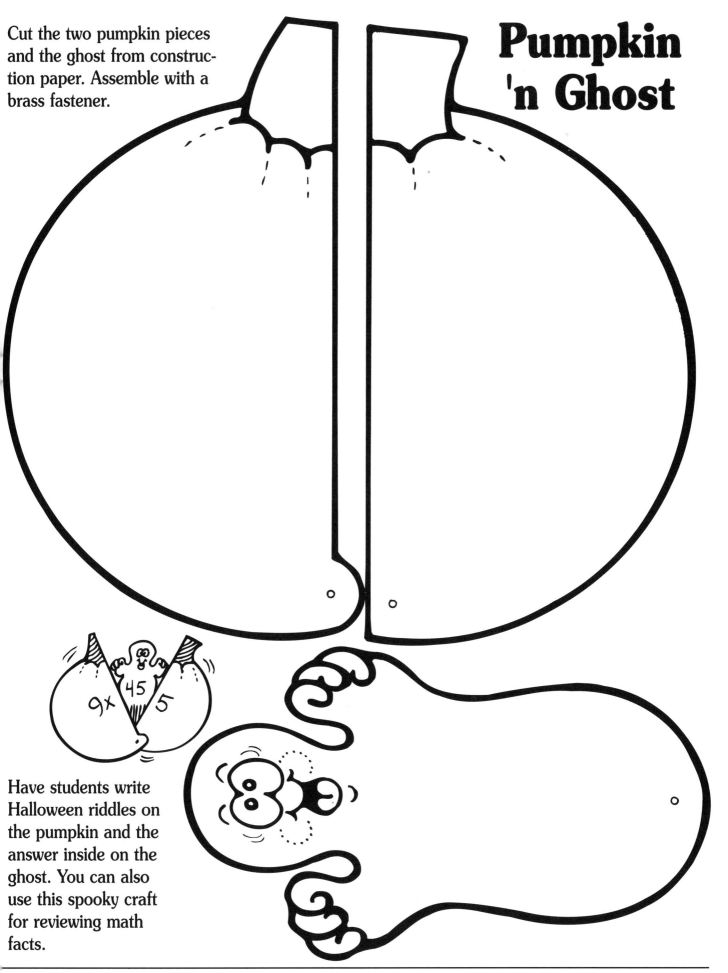

Have students write Halloween riddles on the pumpkin and the answer inside on the ghost. You can also use this spooky craft for reviewing math facts.

Matching Ghosts

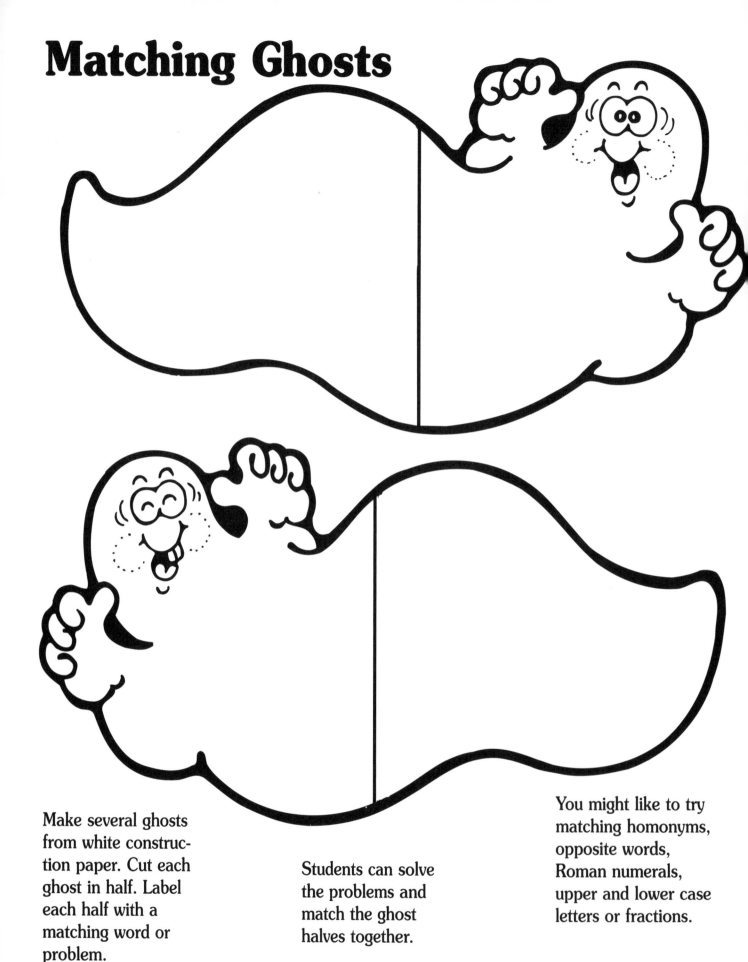

Make several ghosts from white construction paper. Cut each ghost in half. Label each half with a matching word or problem.

Students can solve the problems and match the ghost halves together.

You might like to try matching homonyms, opposite words, Roman numerals, upper and lower case letters or fractions.

Halloween Finger Puppets

cut out

cut out

cut out

cut out

cut out

cut out

cut out

cut out

Students will be eager to complete creative writing assignments with these finger puppets as motivators.

Ask each child to choose a puppet and write a story about it. Students can act out their stories in front of the class.

Use these cute finger puppets as awards for good behavior or completed work.

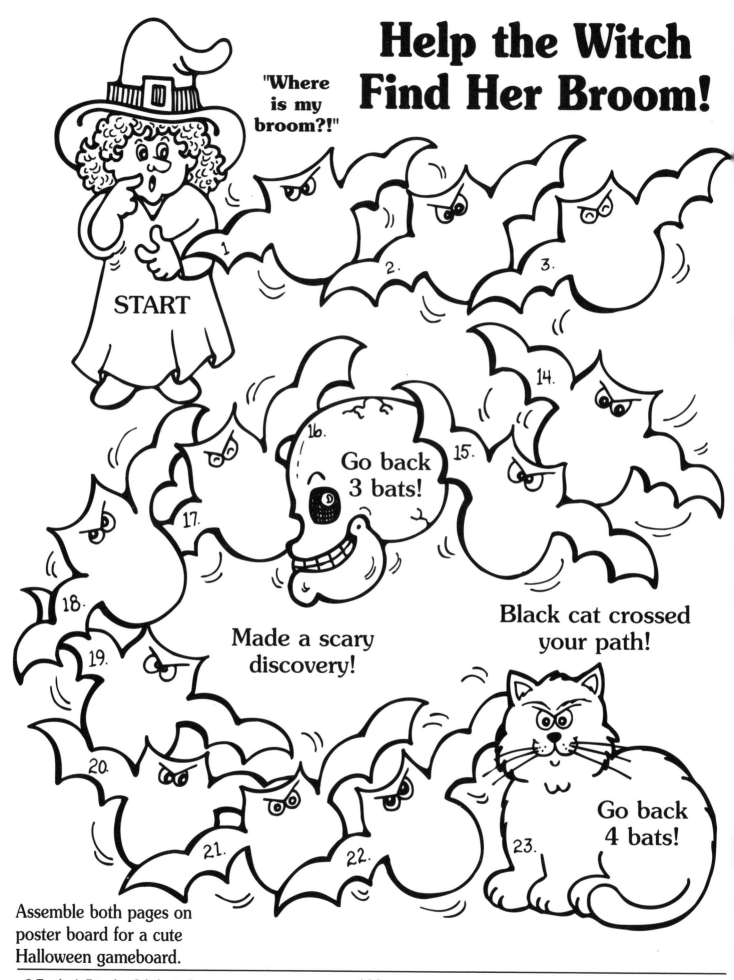

Help the Witch Find Her Broom!

"Where is my broom?!"

START

Go back 3 bats!

Made a scary discovery!

Black cat crossed your path!

Go back 4 bats!

Assemble both pages on poster board for a cute Halloween gameboard.

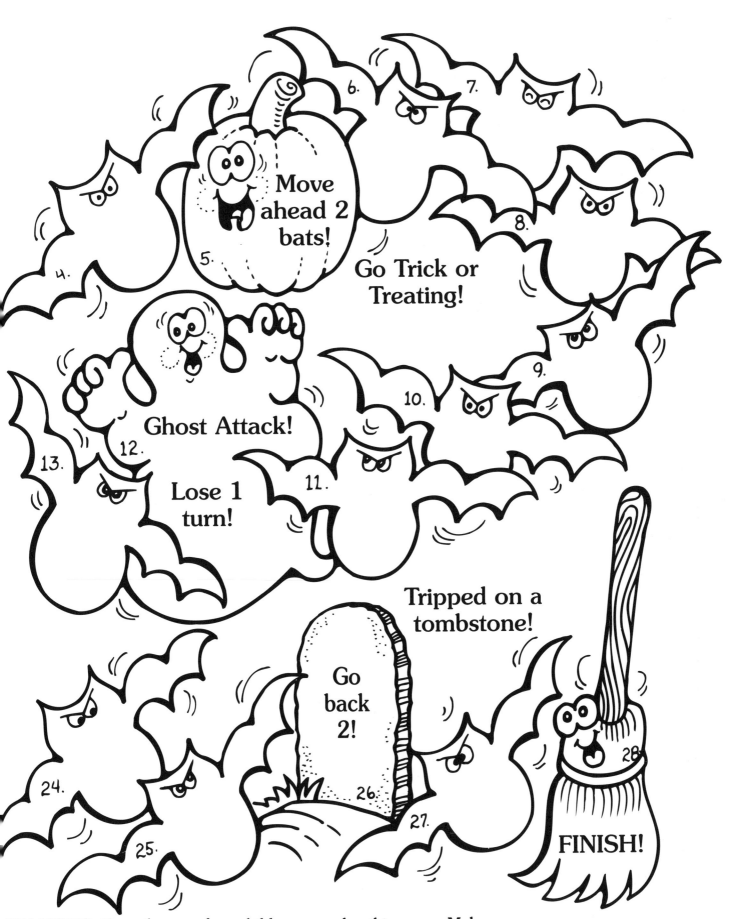

TEACHERS: Two, three or four children can play this game. Make your
own task cards or write math problems, that must be solved, on each bat.

TF1000 October Idea Book

Pumpkin Puppet

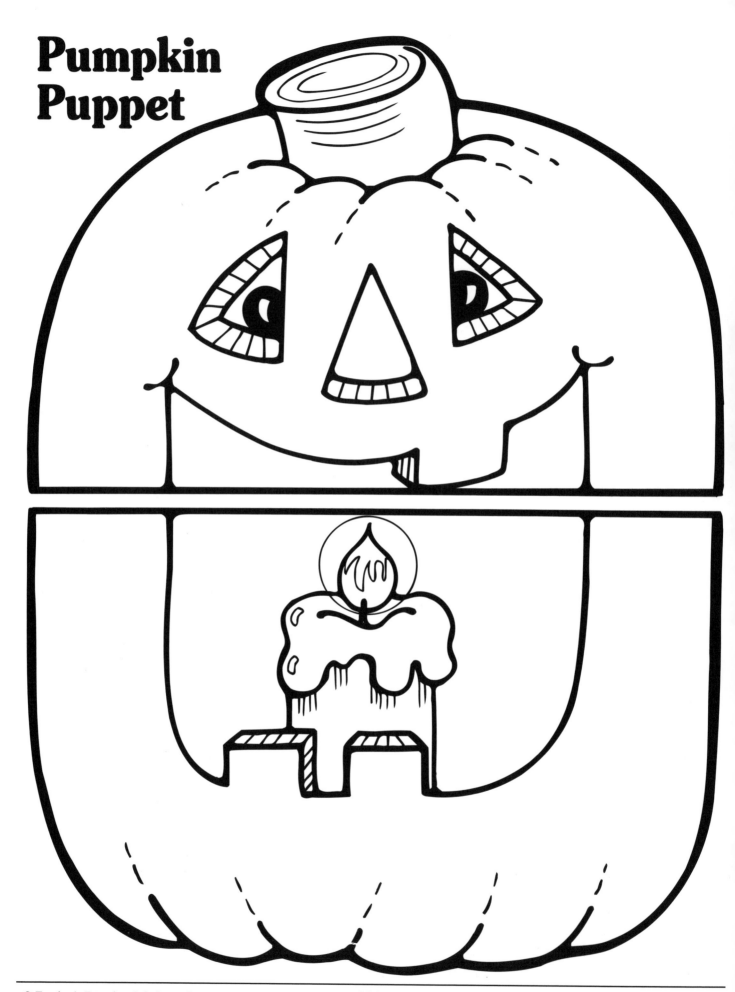

Bat Pattern

Trace this bat pattern onto folded black construction paper and cut out. Fold wings outward along the dotted lines. Hang several bats around the classroom by attaching strings to the center of each bat's body.

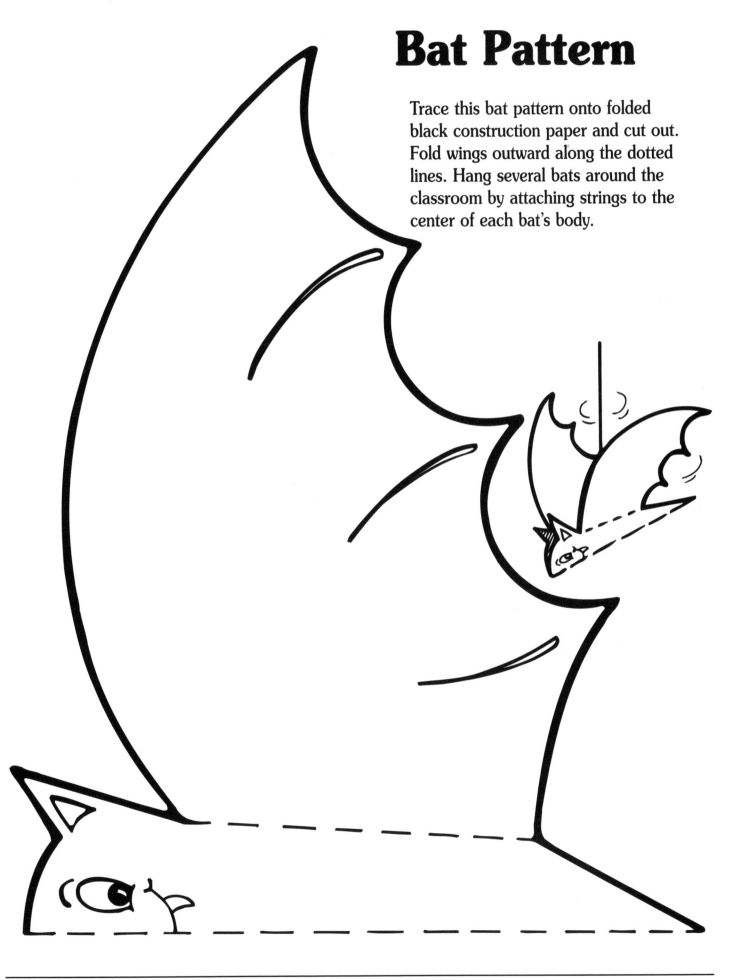

Ghost Wheel

Cut out and assemble this Ghost Wheel with a brass fastener. Cut out the two rectangles, as shown.

Add your own math problems and answers to the wheel on the next page. Move the pumpkin to reveal the answer.

Cut out

Cut out

Make a "Ghost Wheel" for each child in class. They will love using this fun method to learn their multiplication tables.

"Scaredy" Cats

Ask your students to write scary stories. You may want to read them a couple of short ghost stories to get them started.

Cut these patterns from black and white construction paper and mount them behind the stories.

Halloween Safety Tips

- Plan your trick-or-treat route ahead of time. Pick streets that are well lit and have neighbors that you know.

- Take a parent, or an older sister or brother with you when you go trick-or-treating. If someone older cannot go with you, then go with a group.

- Trick-or-treat when it is still light outside, if possible.

- Wear a costume that makes it easy for you walk and can be seen after dark.

- Carry a flashlight and use reflective tape on your costume so that people driving cars can see you.

- If you wear a mask, take it off before crossing streets. If possible, wear make-up instead of a mask.

- Cross only at corners. Never cross the street between parked cars or in the middle of a busy block.

- If there are no sidewalks, walk facing oncoming traffic to make sure you can see the cars.

- Do not eat your candy until you get home and an adult can check it over to make sure it's safe.

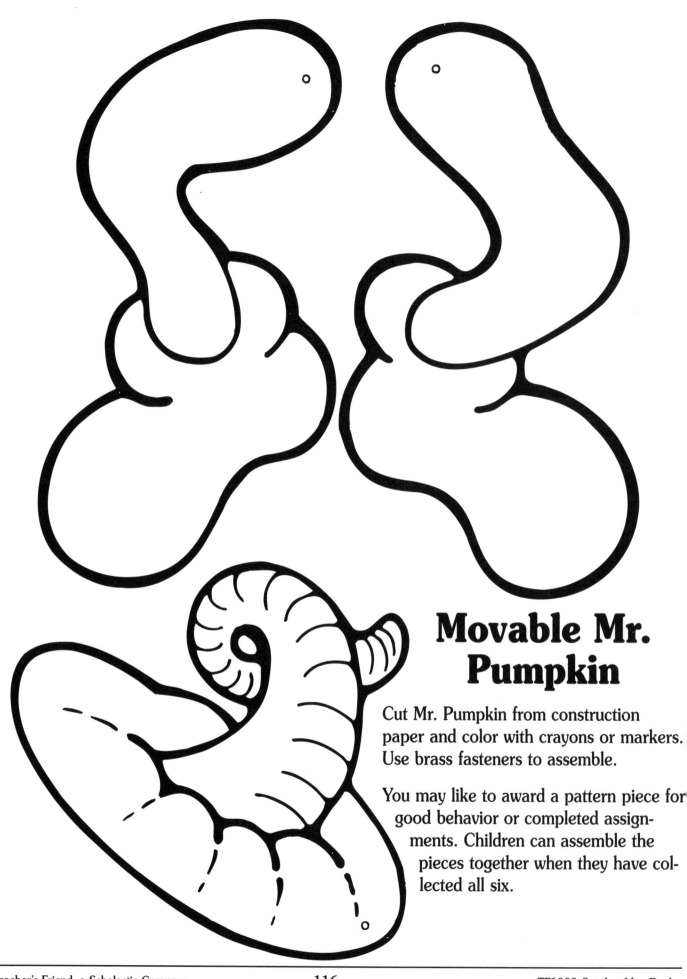

Movable Mr. Pumpkin

Cut Mr. Pumpkin from construction paper and color with crayons or markers. Use brass fasteners to assemble.

You may like to award a pattern piece for good behavior or completed assignments. Children can assemble the pieces together when they have collected all six.

Draw your own
pumpkin face.

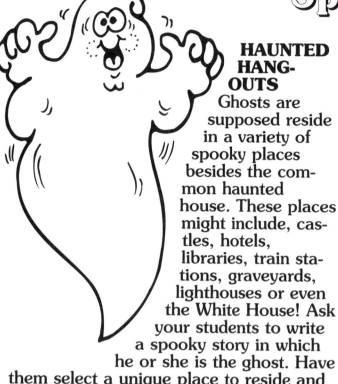

HAUNTED HANG-OUTS

Ghosts are supposed reside in a variety of spooky places besides the common haunted house. These places might include, castles, hotels, libraries, train stations, graveyards, lighthouses or even the White House! Ask your students to write a spooky story in which he or she is the ghost. Have them select a unique place to reside and tell about their haunting adventure. You might want them to include the answers to these questions in their story.

Why did you pick this place to haunt?
What type of people do you most like to scare? Are you a friendly ghost?
What time of day or night do you usually do your haunting?
How long have you been a ghost?
Do you have a name?
Were you once a famous person? Who?

GHOSTLY BREWS

Ask your students to write recipes for their own "Ghostly Brew!"

Let them use their most ghoulish imaginations but emphasize that they must use accurate measurements with a breakdown of each amount. For example:

BILLY'S BREW OF BAT WINGS

Pour four cups (32 oz.) of powdered bat wings in a large bowl. Add one gallon (4 quarts) of liquid snail slime. Stir gently until the color turns purple. Boil on top of the stove until it reaches 212 degrees Fahrenheit (100 degrees centigrade). Cool and drink between the hours of 11:45 PM and 12:00 midnight!

FAMOUS MONSTERS

Ask your students to brainstorm the names of all the monsters they have either read stories about, seen on television or seen in the movies. Here are some monster names you will hear:

FRANKENSTEIN	WOLF MAN
BIG FOOT	DRACULA
MUMMY	KING KONG
THE THING	THE BLOB
CYCLOPS	LOCH NESS
INVISIBLE MAN	MR. HYDE
THE ALIEN	GODZILLA
SEA SERPENT	RODAN

ABOMINABLE SNOWMAN
HEADLESS HORSEMAN
CREATURE OF BLACK LAGOON

Assign each student a monster and have them find out if the monster is from a famous story, legend or a movie maker's invention. They may want to write a story about their monster from a current perspective. For instance, "What would happen if the Loch Ness Monster turned up in the local swimming pool?"

MONSTROUS STORY

Have your students write a collective monster story in which everyone can participate.

Using the chalkboard or large easel paper, write a spooky line that begins the story, such as, *I looked out my bedroom window and saw a large, dark shadow move across the yard.*

Now, ask a student to add a line to the story. Each child in class adds to the story while you write it down.
When the monstrous adventure is complete, read the entire story through and let the class decide on its title.

Spooky Activities!

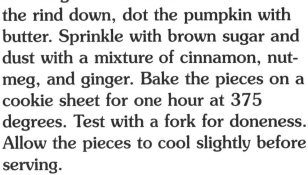

GROUPING PUMPKIN SEEDS

Reinforce number sequencing and grouping with pumpkin seeds.

Assign students to take turns cleaning a large pumpkin. Have them remove the seeds and dry them on paper towels. (Wrap the pumpkin in a damp towel and place it in a refrigerator for an activity the next day.)

Spray a cookie sheet with non-stick cooking spray and bake the seeds at 350 degrees for about twenty minutes. You may like to sprinkle the seeds with salt before baking.

After baking, give each student a paper towel and about 20 seeds. As a class group, have them arrange their seeds in groups of 2's and then 3's, 5's, etc. Give them a variety of simple addition and subtraction problems to solve using the pumpkin seeds. When the lesson is complete, let them eat the seeds.

MONSTER MASH

Ask your students to create a variety of ghoulish recipes. Suggestions could include, monster mash, ghoul garnish, coffin casserole, spooky salad, poltergeist pasta, vampire veggies, etc.

You might also want to bring in a recording of the golden oldie, "Monster Mash." This would be a perfect time to teach them to dance the "mash" along with other favorites like "the jerk" and "twist!"

YUMMY PUMPKIN

Let your students sample a pumpkin treat without going through the hassle of making pumpkin pies.

Using the pumpkin saved from the "grouping" activity, cut it into four large sections. With the rind down, dot the pumpkin with butter. Sprinkle with brown sugar and dust with a mixture of cinnamon, nutmeg, and ginger. Bake the pieces on a cookie sheet for one hour at 375 degrees. Test with a fork for doneness. Allow the pieces to cool slightly before serving.

Cut the pieces into smaller chunks and serve them to your students on paper towels. Your students will be surprised how good a real pumpkin can taste!

AUDIO HAUNTINGS

Children love the spooky sounds of the Halloween season. Let them record their own haunting noises that can be played during a spooky writing activity or the class Halloween party.

Divide the class into groups of four or five and have them plan five minutes of recording time. Students can collect a variety of spooky items and ideas that can be used for the recording, such as, rattling chains, fingernails on a chalkboard, crinkled wax paper, moans, heavy breathing, etc. Place a cassette recorder on a table in one corner of the classroom and assign each group time to make their recording. Let students vote for the scariest group recording.

Spooky Activities!

WHO'S AFRAID?

Discuss common childhood fears with your students . Ask them if they have ever been afraid of the dark, or of thunder and lightening. Explain to them the differences between "real" fears and "unrealistic" fears. Have them discuss ways in which they can help eliminate their fears, such as; leaving on a night light or listening to music.

They may want to talk about scary movies they have seen on television. Encourage them to discuss how makeup and special effects can make a scary situation seem real even though none of the actors are ever harmed.

Ask your students to think of things that might make a monster be afraid. Have each child imagine and draw a picture of a monster, and then write a story in which their monster was frightened.

PUMPKIN PATCH

Give each classmate a brown, paper grocery bag. Ask the students to each stuff their bag with crumpled newspaper and tie off the opening with twine. The stuffed bags, or pumpkins, can now be painted with orange tempera paint.

Let the pumpkins dry overnight and instruct the students to add faces with black permanent markers. Encourage them to be creative by making their jack-o-lanterns sad or happy, mean or scary, etc. When pumpkins are complete, place them on a counter in the classroom. Entwine the pumpkins with long strips of green crepe paper and green construction paper leaves.

GHOSTLY CONCENTRATION

Create a fun, "spooky" game with this simple idea! Write each of the following words on two index cards.

GHOST	WITCH	SPOOK
HORROR	GLOOMY	SCARY
MONSTER	DARK	GOBLIN
SPIDER	GRAVE	BOO
CREEPY	FIEND	DEMON
FRIGHTEN	SCREAM	HAUNT

Shuffle the cards and lay them face down on a table top. Students take turns turning over two cards, hoping to make a match. If a student makes a match, he or she gets to keep the cards and takes another turn. If a match is not made, the next player gets a turn. The player with the most cards after all of the cards have been chosen wins the game.

After playing the game, have students randomly select five word cards. Have them write a spooky story using these five words.

GHOST PENCIL TOPPERS

Motivate students in their next writing assignment with this cute and easy treat!

Give each student a cotton ball, a white paper tissue and a 10" length of black yarn. Ask them to place the cotton ball, covered with the tissue, over the top of their longest pencil. Have them tie the yarn around the pencil to hold it in place. With a black magic marker, have them add "spooky" faces to their ghosts.

As an extra special treat, give each student a "Tootsie Pop" instead of a cotton ball. Everyone can eat their treat at the end of the day!

Spooky Activities!

SELF-CORRECTING INVISIBLE GHOSTS

A fun, "spooky" way to motivate students to learning their math facts can easily be done using this simple idea!

Select one of the ghost patterns contained in this unit and copy it several times into three layers of laminating film with a permanent marker. (Feed a long section of laminating film through a hot laminator two times to increase the weight of the lamination.) Students can cut out the ghosts and draw on scary faces.

On half of the ghosts, write math problems with a permanent marker. On the second half, write the correct answers to the problems. Have students match up the two ghosts by placing the question ghost on top of the answer ghost. Students will be able to see the answers through the top of the invisible "ghost!"

Students can also use "invisible" ghosts in creative writing assignments. Have the children write spooky riddles on the ghosts with a permanent marker. Students can trade riddles and write in their own riddle answers with a dry transfer marker. The answers can then be erased and answered over and over again!

3-D HALLOWEEN CHARACTERS

Cut the patterns on the next two pages from construction paper. Fold each of the characters along the vertical dotted line. With scissors, cut along the horizontal lines. Carefully open the characters. Make the characters three-dimensional by pushing one strip forward and the next backward. Alternate the strips in this way until you have done them all. Attach a piece of yarn to the top and hang in the classroom.

You may want to have students write spooky vocabulary words on the strip sections before cutting.

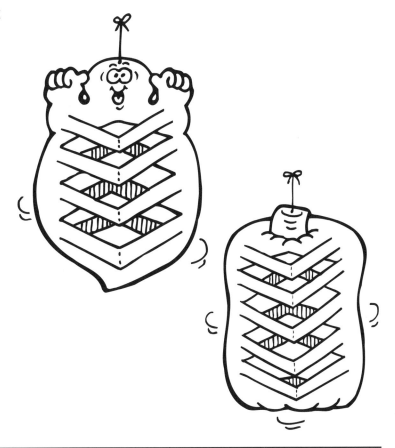

3-D Ghost

FOLD

3-D Pumpkin

FOLD

Cat Tails

(Note: eyes, nose and ears can be cut from white and pink paper and glued in place.)

Cut this cat pattern from black paper.

TF1000 October Idea Book

Cat Tail

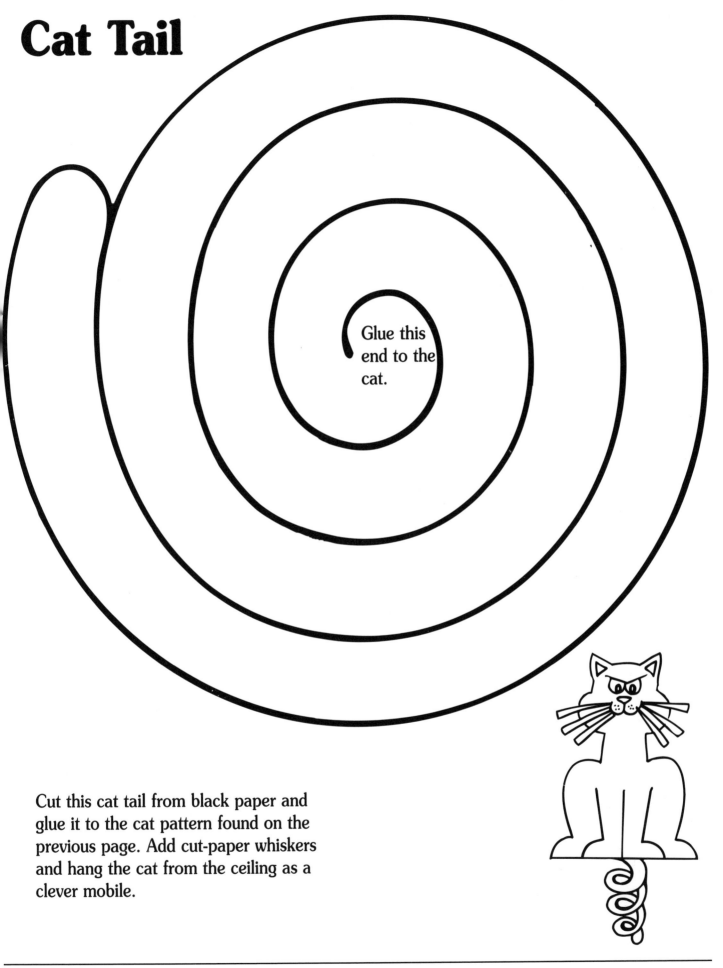

Glue this
end to the
cat.

Cut this cat tail from black paper and
glue it to the cat pattern found on the
previous page. Add cut-paper whiskers
and hang the cat from the ceiling as a
clever mobile.

Make A Monster!

eyes

Have students select monster features and then create their own monster by adding hair, ears, etc.

noses

Students can write creative stories about their monsters.

TF1000 October Idea Book

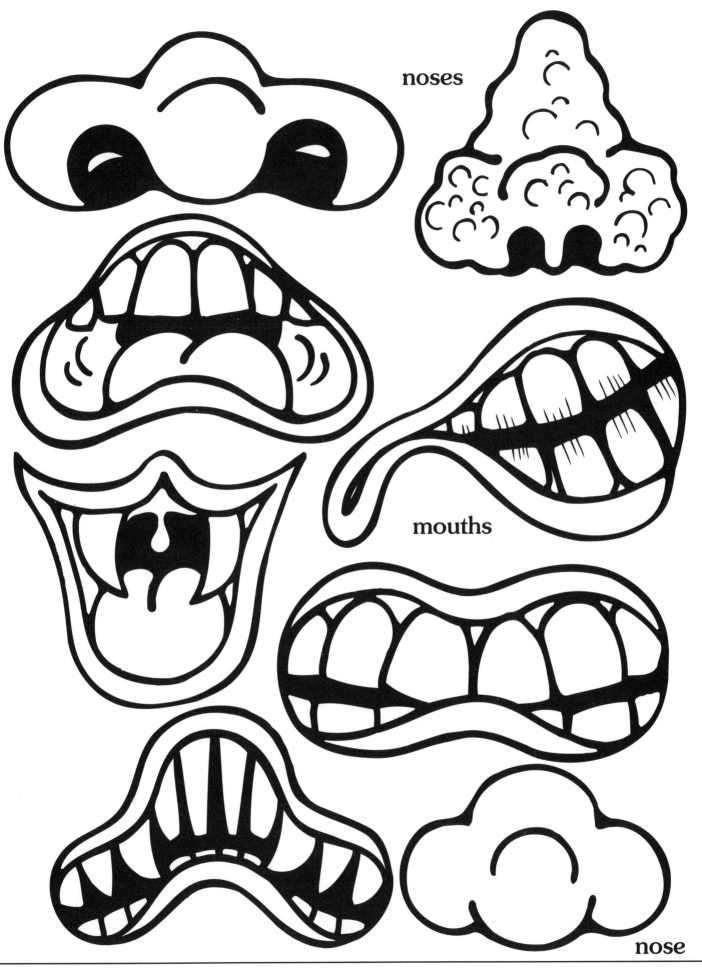

noses

mouths

nose

Creative Writing Page

Bulletin Boards and more!

Look Whoooo's Special!

Anna · Lucinda · Richie · Holly · Jose · Krista · Thomas

TF1000 October Idea Book

Bulletin Boards and More!

OUR READING PATCH

Display a large orange pumpkin for each student on the class bulletin board. As assignments are completed or stories read, the students add eyes, noses and mouths to their pumpkins, which quickly turn into jack-o-lanterns.

WHOOOOOOO KNOWS?

Enlarge this "wise" owl onto poster board and display it in the center of a bulletin board. Cut pictures of famous people and places from magazines and periodicals and arrange them around the owl. Ask students to identify each picture and award the student with the most correct answers.

WHICH IS WITCH?

Students will love studying homonyms with this clever bulletin board. Display a large Halloween witch in one corner. Write different homonyms on strips of colored paper and place them around the board. Children can match up the words when work is completed.

Bulletin Boards and More!

FANG-TASTIC

Take the "bite" out of school work by displaying Dracula on the class bulletin board. Cover the board with black paper. Place Dracula's face and hands above the board, as shown. Children will be eager to see their papers displayed in such a "fang-tastic!" way.

SPOOKY MURAL

Everyone in class will love adding their own touches to this "spooky" mural. Cover the board with black paper and have children cut haunted houses and flying ghosts from paper. Colored chalk can be used to add details.

GHOST WRITERS

Have students write "ghostly" stories on white paper ghost cut-outs. Display ghosts on the class bulletin board omitting each author's name. Children will have fun guessing the identity of each "ghost" writer.

Bulletin Boards and More!

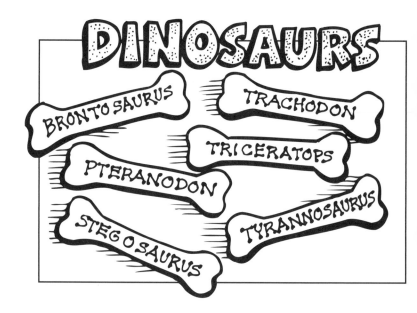

BONE UP ON DINOSAURS

Display dinosaur names on large paper bones cut from white construction paper. Students can list dinosaur facts under the names, along with drawings of each dinosaur.

HARVEST OF GOOD WORK

Children will enjoy collecting fall leaves for this autumn bulletin board. Pin the actual leaves around the board or cut paper leaves for the good work papers. (You may wish to laminate the leaves first.) Write the owners' names on the paper leaves with colored markers.

FIREPROOF YOUR HOME

Instruct students on the value of fire prevention with the help of this fire safety bulletin board. After the class discussion, list items that should be checked to insure a fire-safe home. Display this list on the board along with a cut-out paper match or fire extinguisher.

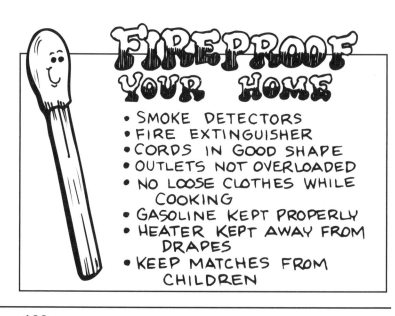

FIREPROOF YOUR HOME

- SMOKE DETECTORS
- FIRE EXTINGUISHER
- CORDS IN GOOD SHAPE
- OUTLETS NOT OVERLOADED
- NO LOOSE CLOTHES WHILE COOKING
- GASOLINE KEPT PROPERLY
- HEATER KEPT AWAY FROM DRAPES
- KEEP MATCHES FROM CHILDREN

Bulletin Boards and More!

WHOOOO AM I?

Cut pictures from magazines and newspapers depicting historical places and heroic people. Mount the pictures on the class board. During free time, have your students use their research skills to identify the people and places in the pictures. Students who can identify all of the pictures receive an award. Change the pictures each week to continue your students' "wise" education.

LOOK WHAT'S POPPING!

Display a cut paper pot and lid on the class bulletin board. Give each student a large, paper popcorn kernel and have them write their name on it. Display the kernels around the pot. (Popcorn pattern shown on page 36.) Paste real popcorn kernels to each student's individual popped corn for completed work or improved behavior.

PUMPKIN PATCH!

Cover the top of the board with black paper. Add purple hills, yellow fields and a white picket fence. Award orange paper pumpkins to students who complete specific tasks. Change the scene by having students draw jack-o-lantern faces on their pumpkins. Corn stalks, scarecrows, owls, bats and a moon can all be added as the season progresses. After Halloween, remove the spooky characters and replace them with pilgrims and horns of plenty.

Bulletin Boards and More!

SPOOKY EPITAPHS!

Inspire your students with this fun display depicting spooky epitaphs!

Have children write silly epitaphs on the tombstone pattern contained in this unit and create a spooky graveyard scene on the class bulletin board. Each epitaph should be written as a rhyme. Using the ghost pattern, students can write ghost stories about the fictional character depicted on their tombstone!

AUTUMN LEAVES

Display a large, bare tree made from brown butcher paper on the class board. Award students red, yellow and orange paper leaves when work is completed and behavior improved. Write the date, task completed or each student's name on the awarded leaf. Children will be eager to earn the leaves and pin them to the tree. You may want to title the display "Autumn Awards!"

DINO-MITE DINOSAURS!

Give each student his or her own dinosaur pattern and ask them to display the patterns on the class board. Children can earn dinosaur "scales" and paste them on to the back of the stegosaurus.

The dinosaur pattern can also be used to denote classroom monitors or reading groups. Simply print the name of each group on the dinosaur and label the scales with the students' names. Scales can be moved as kids move from group to group.

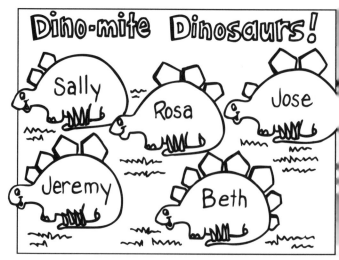

Bulletin Boards and More!

SPOOKY HEADINGS

Tear letters from white paper for a "spooky" effect. Letters can also be cut from rolled cotton or crumpled pieces of plastic wrap.

ROAD MAP LETTERS

Large letters cut from old road maps will add interest to a bulletin board on mapping skills.

NAME THAT TUNE

Cut headline letters from old sheet music or pages from discarded song books.

STYROFOAM HEADLINES

Cut letters form styrofoam sheets. This is a great way to announce the coming of winter or a unit on Alaska.

CURRENT EVENTS

Get students' attention by displaying headlines cut from real newspaper headlines or from classified ad pages.

FEATHERED FRIENDS

A bulletin board announcing a unit on birds will literally jump off the wall with the letters written in real feathers.

RED, WHITE AND BLUE

Celebrate patriotic themes by cutting letters from red, white and blue striped wrapping paper.

Witch Pattern

Pumpkin Face Patterns

Fang-tastic Dracula

This Dracula pattern can also be given to each student. Mounted and colored on a large sheet of construction paper, it can display spooky stories in a dramatic way.

Enlarge Dracula for a "fang"-tastic, over the top bulletin board display.

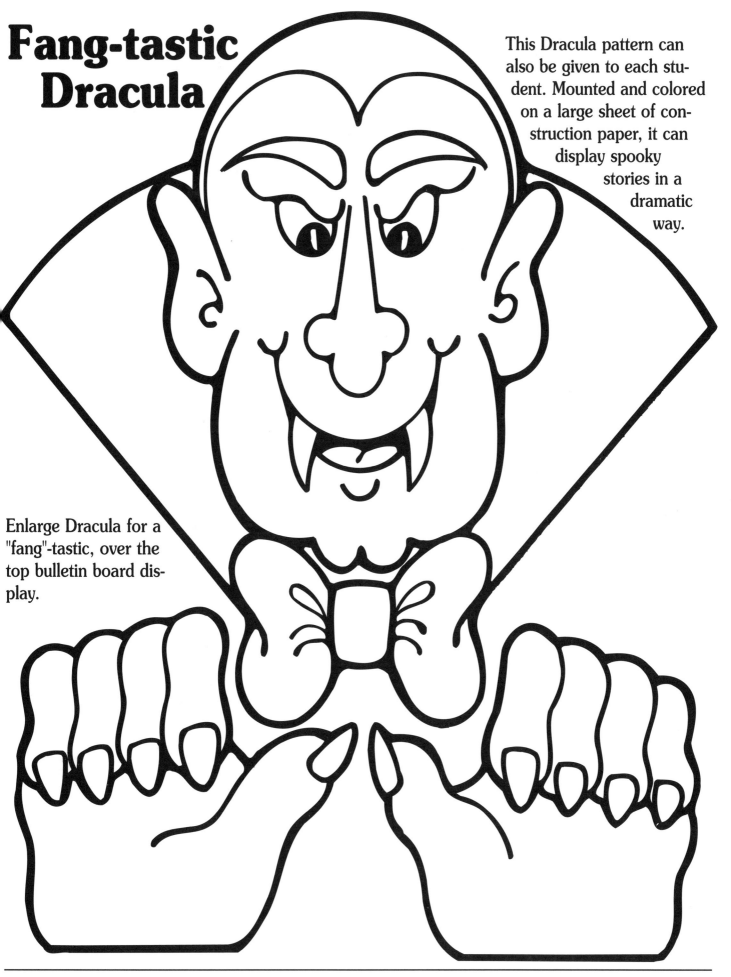

Creative Writing Ghost

TF1000 October Idea Book

Haunted House Pattern

Enlarge this haunted house for a spooky bulletin board display. Children can add the finishing touches, including pumpkins, ghosts and other scary characters at the windows.

Tombstone

R.I.P.
REST - IN - PEACE

Write a funny epitaph.

TF1000 October Idea Book

Dinosaur Pattern

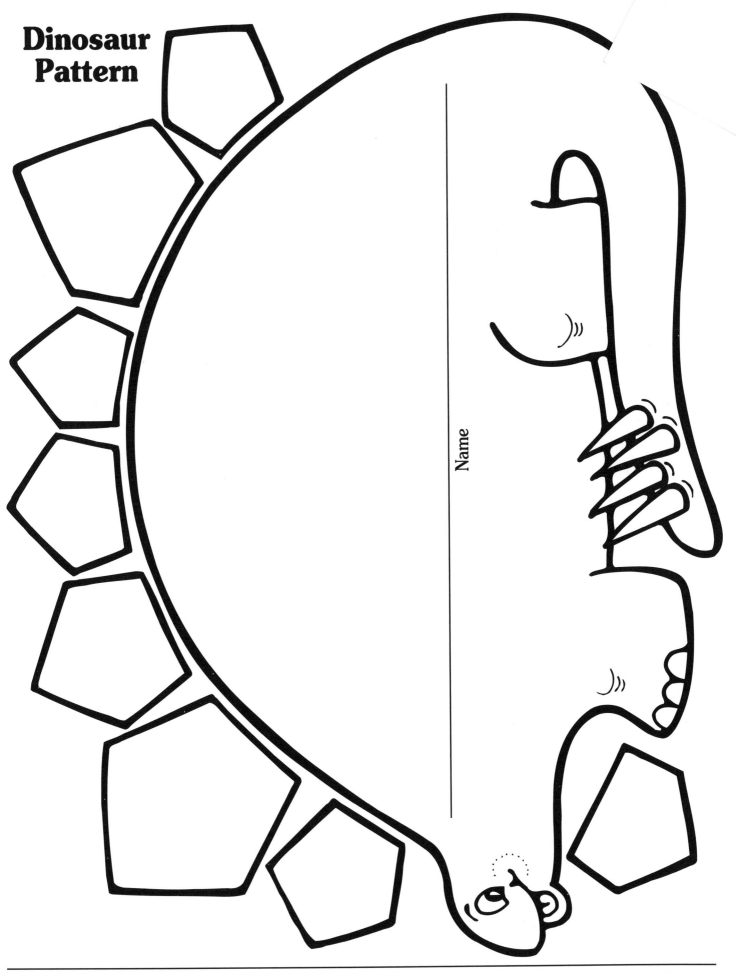

Name

TF1000 October Idea Book

Bare Tree Pattern

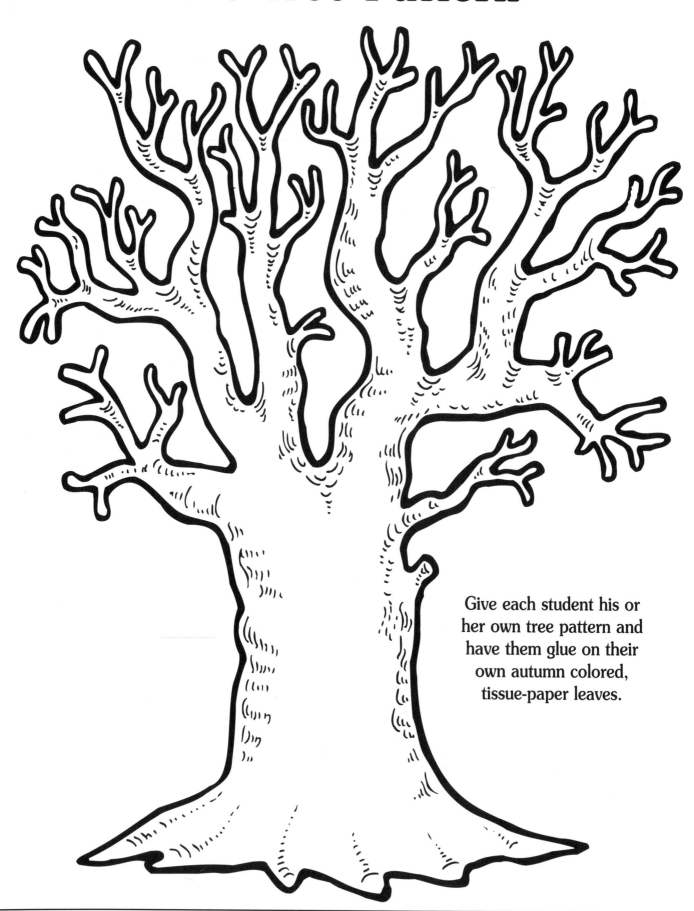

Give each student his or her own tree pattern and have them glue on their own autumn colored, tissue-paper leaves.